Emergence:
Morphogenetic Design Strategies

Guest-edited by Michael Hensel, Achim Menges and Michael Weinstock
of the Emergence and Design Group

Architectural Design
Vol 74 No 3 May/June 2004

Editorial Offices
International House
Ealing Broadway Centre
London W5 5DB
T: +44 (0)20 8326 3800
F: +44 (0)20 8326 3801
E: architecturaldesign@wiley.co.uk

Editor
Helen Castle
Production
Mariangela Palazzi-Williams
Art Director
Christian Küsters (CHK Design)
Project Coordinator
and Picture Editor
Caroline Ellerby

Advertisement Sales
01243 843272

Editorial Board
Will Alsop, Denise Bratton,
Adriaan Beukers, André Chaszar,
Peter Cook, Teddy Cruz,
Max Fordham, Massimiliano Fuksas,
Edwin Heathcote, Anthony Hunt,
Charles Jencks, Jan Kaplicky,
Robert Maxwell, Jayne Merkel,
Monica Pidgeon, Antoine Predock,
Michael Rotondi, Leon van Schaik,
Kenneth Yeang

Contributing Editors
André Chaszar
Craig Kellogg
Jeremy Melvin
Jayne Merkel

ISBN 0-470-86688-8
Profile No 169

Abbreviated positions:
b=bottom, c=centre, l=left, r=right

Front and back cover: © Emergenze
and Design Group

𝐀𝐃

p 4 © WG/Science Photo Library; pp 6(t) & 7 © Pascal Goetgheluck/Science Photo Library; p 6(b) © Emergence and Design Group; pp 10-11 © Nasa/Science Photo Library; pp 12-13 © Martin Dohrn/Science Photo Library; p 14 © George Post/Science Photo Library; p 16 from D'Arcy Wentworth Thompson, On Growth and Form: The Complete Revised Edition, Dover Publications; pp 18, 21, 22 & 25 © ILEK – Institut für Leichtbau Entwerfen und Konstruieren, Universität Stuttgart; pp 20, 23 & 24 © The Emergence and Design Group; pp 26- 33 © Michael Hensel, OCEAN NORTH; pp 34-9 © FOA; pp 40-6 © Emergence and Design Group; p 47 © Neri Oxman; pp 48-53 © Achim Menges; p 53(bl) © Achim Menges, photo Sue Barr; pp 54 & 58-9 © Lina Martinson; pp 62-3 © Sylvia Felipe & Jordi Truco; pp 64-71 © Arup; pp 72-9 © Waagner Biro Stahl-Glas-Technik; pp 80-9 © Achim Menges; p 88(c) © Achim Menges, photo Sue Barr; pp 90-1 © Prof P Motta/Dept Anatomy/University 'La Sapienza', Rome/Science Photo Library; p 93 Andrew Syred/Science Photo Library; p 94 (tl) © Claude Nurisany & Marie Perennou/Science Photo Library; p 94 (tr) © WG/Science Photo Library; p 95 © KR Porter/Science Photo Library.

pp 106-10 & 112 © Paul Gosney; p 111 © Trevor Mein/Mein Photo; p 113 © Dale Jones-Evans; pp 114-16 © Foster and Partners, photos Nigel Young; p 117 © Foster and Partners; p 119 © Eleanor Curtis; pp 122-3 & 124(t) Cedric Price Archive © Canadian Centre for Architecture, Montreal; p 124(b) © David Greene; pp 126-7 © Gehry International Architects, Inc.

ERRATA CORRIGE Due to a technical error, some of the photocredits published in Gans and Weisz, Extreme Sites, AD vol 74, no 2 were incorrect. The correct photo credits should read as follows: p 91 © Wimmitji Tjapangarti courtesy Aboriginal Artists Agency Sydney and DACS 2004; p 92 © DACS 2004; p 95(r) © NASA, pp 99-100 © Jeff Goldberg/Esto

𝐀𝐃+

pp 98-100 © Dan Klores Communications; pp 101 & 104(tl) © Colin Fournier; p 104(bl) from Bild und Tonarchiv, Landesmuseum Joanneum; p 104 (tr & br) © Monika Nikolic; p 105 © Niki Lackner;

Subscription Offices UK
John Wiley & Sons Ltd.
Journals Administration Department
1 Oldlands Way, Bognor Regis
West Sussex, PO22 9SA
T: +44 (0)1243 843272
F: +44 (0)1243 843232
E: cs-journals@wiley.co.uk

Annual Subscription Rates 2004
Institutional Rate: UK £175
Personal Rate: UK £99
Student Rate: UK £70
Institutional Rate: US $270
Personal Rate: US $155
Student Rate: US $110
𝐀𝐃 is published bi-monthly.
Prices are for six issues and include postage and handling charges. Periodicals postage paid at Jamaica, NY 11431. Air freight and mailing in the USA by Publications Expediting Services Inc, 200 Meacham Avenue, Elmont, NY 11003

Single Issues UK: £22.50
Single Issues outside UK: US $45.00
Details of postage and packing charges available on request

Postmaster
Send address changes to 𝐀𝐃 Publications Expediting Services, 200 Meacham Avenue, Elmont, NY 11003

Printed in Italy. All prices are subject to change without notice. [ISSN: 0003-8504]

06
10
26
48
54
80
90
98+
101+
106+
114+
126+

4   Editorial *Helen Castle*

6   Emergence in Architecture *Emergence and Design Group*

10   Morphogenesis and the Mathematics of Emergence *Michael Weinstock*

18   Frei Otto in Conversation with the Emergence and Design Group

26   Finding Exotic Form: An Evolution of Form Finding as a Design Method *Michael Hensel*

34   Types, Style and Phylogenesis *Farshid Moussavi and Alejandro Zaera Polo*
     of Foreign Office Architects in conversation with the Emergence and Design Group

40   Fit Fabric: Versatility Through Redundancy and Differentiation *The Emergence and Design Group*

48   Evolutionary Computation and Artificial Life in Architecture: Exploring the Potential of Generative and
     Genetic Algorithms as Operative Design Tools *Dr Una-May O'Reilly, Martin Hemberg and Achim Menges*

54   Drunk in an Orgy of Technology *Professor Chris Wise*

64   Engineering Design: Working with Advanced Geometries *Charles Walker of Arup & Partners*
     in conversation with the Emergence and Design Group

72   Manufacturing Complexity *Johann Sischka of Waagner Biro in conversation with*
     the Emergence and Design Group

80   Morpho-Ecologies: Approaching Complex Environments *Achim Menges*

90   Biodynamics *Professor George Jeronimidis*

96   Biographies

Guest-edited by Michael Hensel, Achim Menges and Michael Weinstock

Emergence:
Morphogenetic Design Strategies

98+   Interior Eye Retail in the Dumpster *Craig Kellogg*

101+   Building Profile The Kunsthaus at Graz *Jeremy Melvin*

106+   Practice Profile Dale Jones-Evans *Leon van Schaik*

114+   Engineering Exegesis Blurring the Lines: The Chesa Futura *André Chaszar*

118+   From Political Reportage to *Prêt-à-Porter* *Eleanor Curtis*

120+   Book Reviews

122+   Supercrit #1 and #2 *Samantha Hardingham*

125+   Book Club

126+   Site Lines: A Sort of Homecoming: The Art Gallery of Ontario *Sean Stanwick*

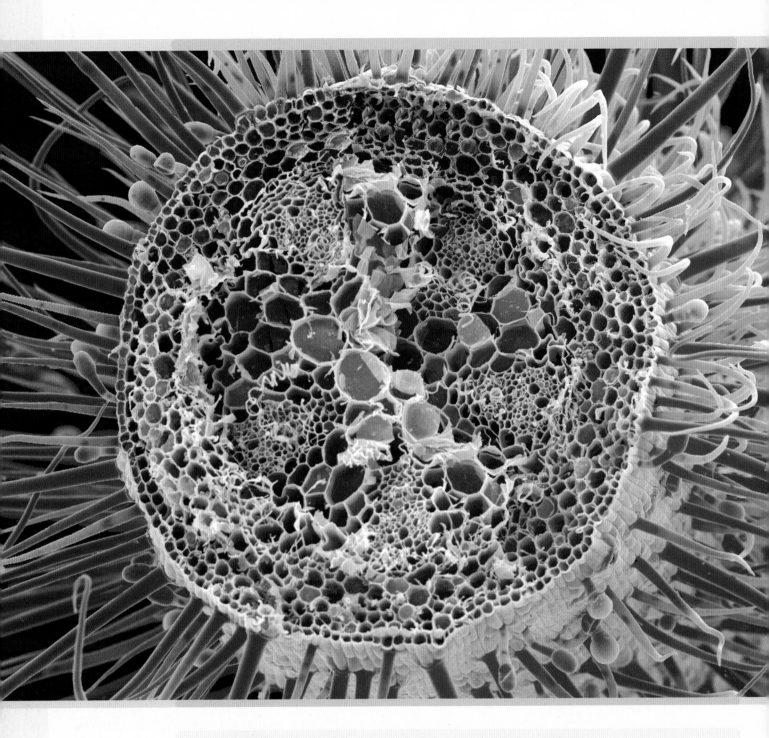

Geometry of Integration and Differentiation in Plant Stem

This section through the stem of a geranium reveals the close-packed bundles of differentiated vessels and specialised cells. The geometrical arrangement and close-packed integration produces a complex structure, strong but flexiblae, and capable of differential movement. All the cells have a structural role in addition to other functions, and structural capacity emerges from their interaction. The large pale tubes in the centre are xylem vessels that transport water and nutrients up from the root. These vessels are reinforced by spiral helices of lignin; the geometry of the spiral helix allows elongation for growth without loss of strength. The five bundles of pale green vessels are phloem cells, part of the vascular system for the distribution of carbohydrates and hormones, and the smaller purple cells on the perimeter are parenchyma cells, which are thin-walled and flexible and can increase or decrease in size by taking up or losing water. These changes cause deformations, which is how the plant achieves movements such as bending towards the light or around an obstacle. The arrangement of cells of different sizes and orientations constrains the movement in the direction that is needed. The stem is enclosed by the epidermis, a double layer of cells, some of which are specialised, with hairs or oil glands.

Editorial Helen Castle

Historically, a wonder of natural systems has served scientists and creative designers well. For example, Leonardo da Vinci's studies of anatomy and the botanical formed the basis for both his art and his inventions. This contrasts sharply with the first half of the 20th century when the motorised machine – whether aeronautical or nautical, or a road vehicle – became the model for architecture, as espoused and illustrated by Le Corbusier in his writings. (The photographs of his much-loved machines becoming almost as famous as his buildings.) Placing man's own inventions at the apex of innovation automatically circumscribes the potential of architectural design and built form, as design becomes largely intent on the production of the single, polished set object. What mechanical system can, after all, compare with the complexity, reflexivity and responsive refinement of the geranium stem illustrated opposite?

For the guest-editors of this issue, Michael Hensel, Achim Menges and Michael Weinstock of the Emergence and Design Group, 'emergence' is the scientific mode in which natural systems can be explored and explained in a contemporary context. It provides 'models and processes for the creation of artificial systems that are designed to produce forms and complex behaviour, and perhaps even real intelligence' (p 6). In this brief definition, emergence already surfaces as a model capable of sophisticated reflexive attributes exceeding any mechanistic or static notion of architectural form – one that could perhaps define new levels of interaction and integration within natural ecosystems. As Weinstock points out in his essay (p 10), emergence has previously only ever really existed as a buzzword in architecture and science, being favoured by architectural thinkers and academics more for its resonance of complexity and connotations of the scientific than as a fixed term. In science it has received a much tighter definition as 'the properties of a system that cannot be deduced from its parts'. Emergence can perhaps be most simply evoked in the natural world by the example of ants, which display far more intelligent behaviour as a colony than alone.

Through its advocacy of emergence, the Emergence and Design Group is intentionally setting out to produce a new researched-based model for architectural enquiry. (There may be common formal traits in this work, as suggested by the title of the group's exhibition 'Contours: Evolutionary Strategies for Design' at the Architectural Association (AA) in London in spring 2003, but this is largely by the way.) The research that has been undertaken is as important for its redefinition of architectural working relationships as the iterative techniques and new material models its proposes.

Through the establishment of the Emergent Technologies and Design masters programme at the AA, the Emergence and Design Group has nurtured links with bioengineers, structural engineers, mathematicians and material scientists as well as architects. The contributions to this issue are very much a product of this interdisciplinary approach. This title is primarily important, though, as it announces the international launch of emergence as a comprehensive intellectual programme for architectural design. ∆

Emergence in Architecture

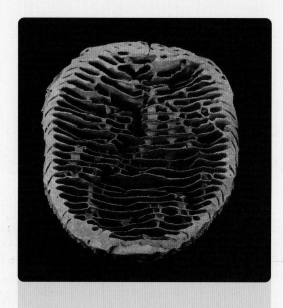

The Emergence
and Design Group

There has been an increasing use of the word 'emergence' in architecture, but as of yet there has not been a systematic investigation of its instruments, nor has there been any real attempt to go beyond the common, but vague, definition of emergence as the properties of a system that cannot be deduced from its parts. Emergence is a consolidation of a paradigm shift that began more than 80 years ago, a profound change that has blurred the boundaries between once quite separate sciences, and which has changed industry. It has made potent changes to the technological world, changes that demand a new way of thinking about architecture and substantial changes to the way we produce it. Emergence does not await a practice and defies conventional categorisation as either theory or practice. Emergence is both an explanation of how natural systems have evolved and maintained themselves, and a set of models and processes for the creation of artificial systems that are designed to produce forms and complex behaviour, and perhaps even real intelligence. The impact of emergence on architecture has significant potential, and an important shift towards the new paradigm and its techniques of evolution and morphogenesis is already under way. This issue of Δ focuses on these methodologies, on experimentation and on the development of new instruments of design.

Emergence and Morphogenesis

It makes little sense to characterise emergence as either solely abstract or purely a means of production; in emergence the two are inextricably intertwined. As used in the sciences, the term refers to the 'emergence' of forms and behaviour from the complex systems of the natural world. A substantial body of knowledge falls under this term, occurring in the overlapping domains of developmental biology, physical chemistry and mathematics.

The techniques and processes of emergence are intensely mathematical and have spread to other domains where the analysis and production of complex forms or behaviour are fundamental. In 'Morphogenesis and the Mathematics of Emergence', Michael Weinstock traces the origins of the concepts and provides an account of the mathematical basis of processes that produce emergent forms and behaviours, in nature and in computational environments. The mathematical models can be used for generating designs, evolving forms and structures in morphogenetic processes within our computational environments.

Morphogenetic strategies for design are not truly evolutionary unless they incorporate iterations of physical modelling, nor can we develop systems that utilise emergence without the inclusion of the self-organising material effects of form finding and the industrial logic of production. Emergence requires the recognition of buildings not as singular and fixed bodies, but as complex energy and material systems that have a life span, and exist as part of the environment of other buildings, and as an iteration of a long series that proceeds by evolutionary development towards an intelligent ecosystem.

Physical form-finding experiments in architecture are thought to have begun with Gaudí. Frei Otto's pioneering work on form finding is well documented and in 'Frei Otto in Conversation with the Emergence and Design Group' he discusses his development of modelling through form-finding techniques in the context of his interest in natural systems, the relation of experimental models to geometry, iterative mathematics and irregularity.

New form-finding methods are needed for the forms capable of change for the adaptation that emergence demands. In 'Finding Exotic Form' Michael Hensel, of OCEAN NORTH, presents the case for a digital and dynamic form-finding technique that suggests a material means of form adaptation in situ. His argument is developed through a design for the World Center for Human Concerns, an architectural study of a 'parasite building' in which structural and circulatory independence from the host is achieved through the skin of the draped volume.

Data, Genes and Speciation

The Emergence and Design Group, founded by Michael Weinstock, Achim Menges and Michael Hensel, present their case for a morphogenetic strategy in the design study of a high-rise building, placed in the context of their argument for integrating structural criteria and behaviour into material systems of vertical urbanism. In 'Fit Fabric' they propose high-rise buildings as surface structures, explore flexure and stiffness, and present models taken from natural structures for geometry, pattern, form and behaviour. Their evolutionary process has produced a design for high-rise structures in which a helical structural system and an intelligent skin are integrated into a versatile material system. The evolutionary technique here is the development of a population of forms from which the fittest is evolved.

The relation of an individual to a population and to a species is a matter of fierce debate, and within developmental biology the argument between Dawkin and Gould has extended for decades. In 'Types, Style and Phylogenesis' Farshid Moussavi and Alejandro Zaera Polo of Foreign Office Architects discuss the systematisation of their work into a phylogram of species, and the implications of this new organisational paradigm regarding the methods and techniques that they have refined during their 10 years in practice. They discuss phylogenesis in the context of reflections on the architectural ideologies of 'type' and 'style', and explain their changing design approach in recent work.

'Emergent Technologies and Design' is a new Master of Architecture programme at the Architectural Association Graduate School, and is the first of its kind in the world. It was developed, and is directed, by Michael Weinstock and Michael Hensel. Achim Menges is the studio master. Professor Chris Wise, director of expedition engineering and chair of civil engineering design at Imperial College, London, is an eminent design engineer, and as external examiner to the

Opposite top and above
Section of complex nest structure built by *Apicotermes* termites: 20 centimetres across, the structure is made from soil and woody material, with external holes to ventilate the horizontal layered passages, which are vertically connected by an internal spiral staircase. The complex form emerges from the collective behaviour of a large number of termites following very simple rules.

Opposite bottom
The Emergence and Design Group. From left to right: Michael Hensel, Michael Weinstock and Achim Menges.

masters programme evaluates the work of the graduating students. In 'Drunk in an Orgy of Technology' he reflects on their intoxication with technology, mathematics and computers, and their pioneering engagement with emergence. A short account of two MA dissertation projects is presented. 'Data-Graphics and Continuous Datasets', by Lina Martinson, explores the digital imaging, mapping and modelling of complex material systems. The increasing currency of complex morphological articulation in contemporary architecture requires the introduction of imaging technologies from medicine and science. 'HybGrid', by Sylvia Felipe and Jordi Truco, is an adaptable structure developed

versions of the genome and the phenome. In 'Evolutionary Computation and Artificial Life in Architecture', Dr Una-May O'Reilly of the Computer Science and Artificial Intelligence Lab at MIT, Martin Hemberg and Achim Menges explore the potential of genetic algorithms as design tools for architecture. The development of 'genetic engines' that model evolutionary and growth processes are demonstrated in the context of two morphogenetic design experiments. The argument for the combination of evolutionary computation with advanced digital modelling and the constraints of manufacturing techniques is developed.

Complex forms in architecture demand new tools and new approaches to design. In 'Engineering Design: Working with Advanced Geometries' Charles Walker,

Emergence Defined

A Mini-Bibliography

1. *Emergence from Chaos to Order*, John Holland, Oxford University Press, 1998

'We are everywhere confronted with emergence in complex adaptive systems – ant colonies, networks of neurons, the immune system, the internet, and the global economy, to name a few – where the behaviour of the whole is much more complex than the behaviour of the parts.'

'... it is unlikely that a topic as complicated as emergence will submit meekly to a concise definition, and I have no such definition to offer. I can, however, provide some markers that stake out the territory, along with some requirements for studying the terrain ...'

Both quotes are from the opening chapter of *Emergence from Chaos to Order*: 'Before We Proceed'. Holland's concentration on well-defined technical concepts as a foundation for a framework for studying emergence is excellent. He explores three kinds of concepts – purely mathematical concepts, systems and games concepts, and general informal concepts. Modelling is central to the book and to his discussion.

through a design strategy that combined digital and material processes. The structure has a multiplicity of stable states that link changing spatial requirements to a corresponding formal and structural articulation. The structure makes use of redundancy and elastic behaviour, which are further explored in the context of the article in 'Adaptable Equilibrium' by Wolf Mangelsdorf of Buro Happold, who also teaches in the Emergent Technologies and Design masters programme. He presents an argument, developed from the study of natural structures, for inbuilt redundancy and multiple load paths as primary requirements for the materialisation of the new concepts of adaptability and controlled dynamics.

Complex forms and systems emerge in nature from evolutionary processes, and their properties are developed incrementally through the processes that work upon successive

leader of the Advanced Geometry Unit (AGU) at Arup & Partners, in conversation with the Emergence and Design Group, discusses AGU's search for a new paradigm, for new organisational principles and the integration of physical and digital modelling in its processes. The collaboration with architects and artists includes Toyo Ito for the Serpentine Gallery Summer Pavilions in 2002, Anish Kapoor for the Marsyas sculpture in the Unilever series at Tate Modern, and David Adjaye for the British Pavilion at the Venice Biennale 2003. Each of these structures required an exploration into the phenomena of the 3-D bracing of interlocking planes, the algorithm as a generative tool, the buckling stability of flat plates, and the manipulation of stressed skins to achieve sculptural form.

Behaviour, Material and Environment
The emphasis on increasing density in mature urban conglomerates is a notable feature in the future strategies of many metropolitan and regional

authorities. When very large numbers of people are concentrated in one place, the resources needed to maintain the environmental quality of public and private spaces increase exponentially. Social interaction is more complex and more intense, and this has to be ameliorated by spatial and infrastructural design that maximises qualitative as well as quantitative factors. Emergence provides models for life cycles, and the way in which different life cycles interact with each other in an ecosystem. This is the key to understanding the ecology of densely occupied environments in which topological, structural and programmatic integration facilitates human activities.

are inextricably intertwined, one acting on the other, and each in turn producing the other. The logic of natural production studied in the sciences of emergence offers a model of seamless integration to replace the conventional separation of design and material production. The search for manufacturing and construction solutions for the complex geometry of contemporary architecture necessitates the development of new methods and tools, and this in turn demands the seamless integration of digital modelling and computer-aided manufacturing. Waagner Biro is the manufacturing contractor best known for complex geometry constructions. In 'Manufacturing Complexity', Johann Sischka, in conversation with the Emergence and Design Group, discusses the construction strategies and methods

2. *Emergence, the Connected Lives of Ants, Brains, Cities and Software*, Steven Johnson, Scribner, 2001 (US); Allan Lane, Penguin Press, 2001 (UK)

In discussion of complex, adaptive systems:

'The movement from low-level rules to higher-level sophistication is what we call emergence', and '... a higher-level pattern arising out of parallel complex interactions between local agents'.

This is a good general read, covering many fields. In particular the second section, covering what Johnson identifies as the four principles of emergence – local interaction of neighbours, pattern recognition, feedback and indirect control – are a good, if general, introduction. The book also offers a short history of the intellectual development of what Johnson calls 'the bottom-up mindset'.

3. 'Self-Organisation, Emergence and the Architecture of Complexity', Francis Heylighen in *Proceedings of the 1st European Conference on System Science*, Paris

'Emergence is a classical concept in systems theory, where it denotes the principle that the global properties defining higher order systems or "wholes" (eg boundaries, organisation, control ...) can in general not be reduced to the properties of the lower order subsystems or "parts". Such irreducible properties are called emergent.'

'The spontaneous creation of an "organised whole" out of a "disordered" collection of interacting parts, as witnessed in self-organising systems in physics, chemistry, biology, sociology ... is a basic part of dynamical emergence.'

This interesting paper concentrates on the dynamics and evolution of emergent properties.

In 'Morpho-Ecologies' Achim Menges presents two of his architectural research projects that explore the dynamic relations and behaviour of occupation patterns, environmental modulations and material systems.

In natural systems most sensing, decision-making and reactions are entirely local, and global behaviour is the product of local actions, with a high degree of functionality in the material itself. All natural material systems involve movement, often without muscles, to achieve adaptation and responsiveness. In 'Biodynamics' Professor George Jeronimidis examines natural dynamic systems, the material behaviour that enables adaptation, and presents the case for implementation of these models in architecture and engineering.

In natural morphogenesis the information or data of the genome and the physical materials drawn from the environment for the phenome

of complex geometry structures, such as the dome of the German Reichstag and the roof of the Sony Center in Berlin, and the roof of the Great Court of the British Museum in London.

This issue could be divided in three sections which delineate the strategy for this initial exploration of emergence in architecture. In the first section, 'Emergence and Morphogenesis', the mathematical techniques for modelling the emergence of forms and behaviour from the complex systems of the natural world are juxtaposed with form-finding techniques for stable and dynamic material forms. In the second section, 'Data, Genes and Speciation', the focus is on geometry, pattern and behaviour, and the computational and material evolution of 'populations' and 'species' of architectural forms with complex behaviour. The third section, 'Behaviour, Material and Environment', is concentrated on the adaptive behaviour of natural and architectural material systems and the industrial potential for a seamless integration of their design and production. ∆

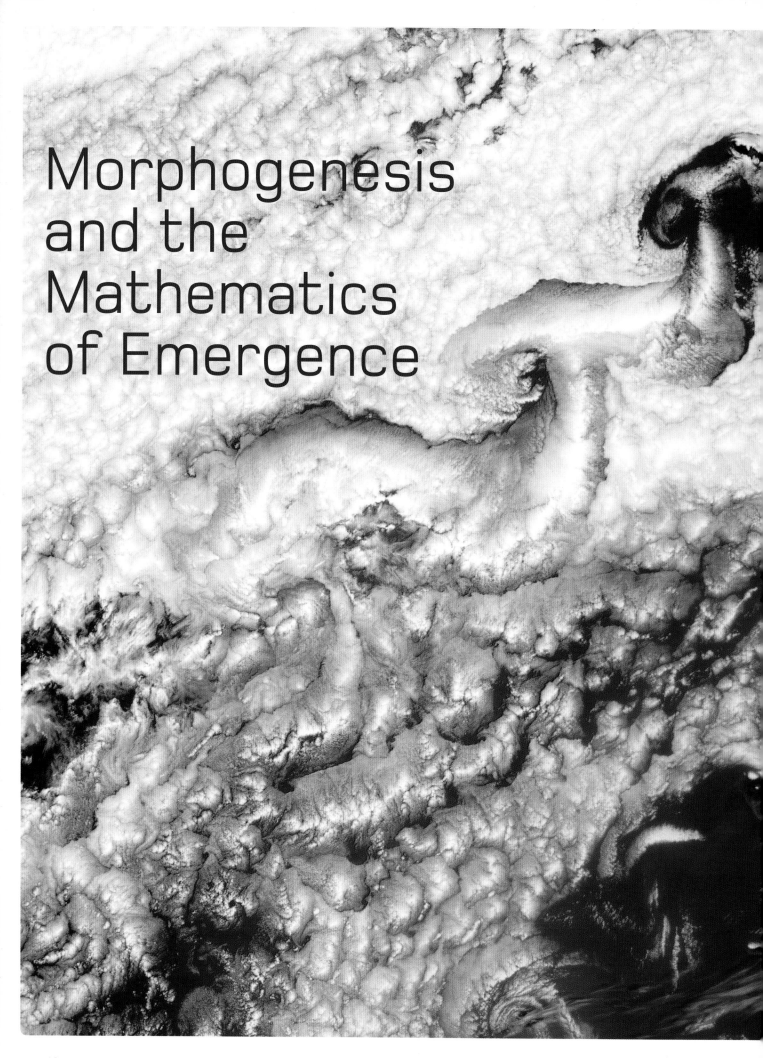

Morphogenesis and the Mathematics of Emergence

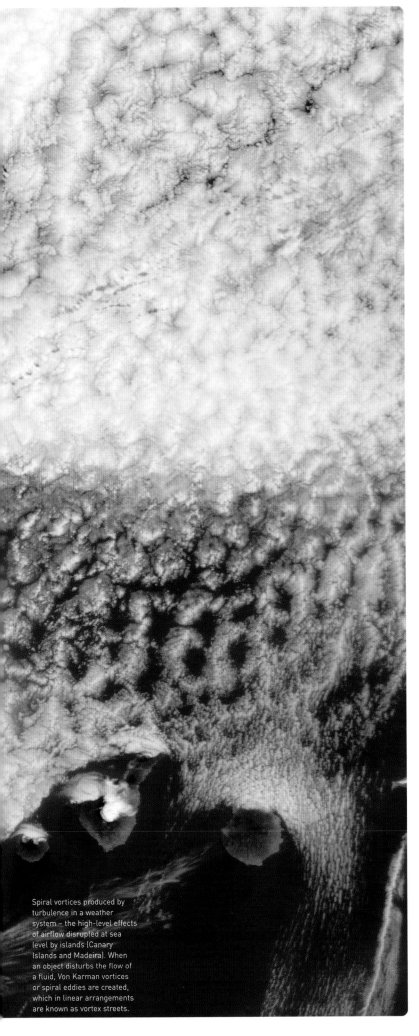

Spiral vortices produced by turbulence in a weather system – the high-level effects of airflow disrupted at sea level by islands (Canary Islands and Madeira). When an object disturbs the flow of a fluid, Von Karman vortices or spiral eddies are created, which in linear arrangements are known as vortex streets.

In this article, Michael Weinstock of the Emergence and Design Group reviews the mathematical basis of processes that produce emergent forms and behaviours, in nature and in computational environments. He presents an argument for a more comprehensive mathematical approach in architecture, in the context of a review of the origins and instruments of emergence in biology, physical chemistry and mathematics. The architectural consequences of this paradigm are outlined.

Emergence is a concept that appears in the literature of many disciplines, and is strongly correlated to evolutionary biology, artificial intelligence, complexity theory, cybernetics and general systems theory. It is a word that is increasingly common in architectural discourse, where too often it is used to conjure complexity but without the attendant concepts and mathematical instruments of science. In the simplest commonly used definition, emergence is said to be the properties of a system that cannot be deduced from its components, something more than the sum of its parts. This description is perhaps true in a very general sense, but rather too vague to be useful for the purpose of design research in architecture. One can truthfully say, for example, that every higher-level physical property can be described as a consequence of lower-level properties. In the sciences, the term refers to the production of forms and behaviour by natural systems that have an irreducible complexity, and also to the mathematical approach necessary to model such processes in computational environments.

The task for architecture is to delineate a working concept of emergence and to outline the mathematics and processes that can make it useful to us as designers. This means we must search for the principles and dynamics of organisation and interaction, for the mathematical laws that natural systems obey and that can be utilised by artificially constructed systems. We should start by asking: What is it that emerges, what does it emerge from, and how is emergence produced?

Mathematics has always played a critical role in architecture, but the character and function of mathematics in relation to the theories and the material objects of architecture have varied so that

Above
Ammonites – fossil shells of small aquatic molluscs. The geometrical organisation of the multichambered shell is a spiral helix.

a definitive account remains elusive. It is evident that there is a pressing need for a more developed mathematical approach in current architecture. First, the liberation of tectonics from the economic straitjacket of orthogonal geometry demands more precision in the interface between architectural definitions of form and the computer-driven fabrication processes of manufacturing constructors. Second, the engineering design for the complex geometries of contemporary tectonics must begin from a definitive mathematical base. And third, there is a lacuna in the theoretical body of architecture, an absence that is marked by the proliferation of design processes that borrow the appearance of scientific methods yet lack their clarity of purpose, mathematical instruments and theoretical integrity.

There is an intricacy in the interchange of ideas and techniques between the disciplines of biology, physical chemistry and mathematics.[1] They are separate, almost discrete but overlapping, and the boundaries between them are indeterminate. The originating concepts and the subsequent development of emergence are founded in these interchanges.

Process and Form
Living organisms can be regarded as systems, and these systems acquire their complex forms and patterns of behaviour through the interactions, in space and over time, of their components. The dynamics of the development of biological forms, the accounts of growth and form, of morphogenesis, have become much more central to evolutionary theory than in Darwin's thesis. Darwin argued that just as

humans breed living organisms by unnatural selection, organising systematic changes in them, so wild organisms themselves are changed by natural selection. Natural selection is a process involving predators and parasites, and environmental pressures such as food supply, temperature and water. Successful organisms will survive the fierce competition and have greater breeding success and, in turn, their offspring will have greater reproductive success, and so on. Darwin's arguments had a remarkable alignment with the then current theory of competitive struggle in capitalism[2] and the concepts of mechanisms in industry. Theories of morphogenesis, the creation of forms that evolve in space and over time, are now inextricably entwined with the mathematics of information theory, with physics and chemistry, and with organisation and geometry. The pattern of alignment with concepts and technologies of economics and industry remains consistent.

The convergent lines of thought between biology and mathematics were initiated early in the 20th century, particularly in the work of Whitehead and D'Arcy Thompson. D'Arcy Thompson, zoologist and mathematician, regarded the material forms of living things as a diagram of the forces that have acted on them.[3] His observations of the homologies between skulls, pelvises and the body plans of different species suggested a new mode of analysis, a mathematisation of biology. Morphological measurements are specific to species and at times to individuals within a species, and so are various, but there are underlying relations that do not vary – the 'homologies'.

Homology has two distinct but related meanings: to biologists it means organs or body parts that have the same evolutionary origin but quite different functions; and to mathematicians it is a classification of geometric figures according to their properties. Form can be described by mathematical data, mapping

The mathematician and philosopher Whitehead argued that process rather than substance was the fundamental constituent of the world, and that nature consists of patterns of activity interacting with each other. Organisms are bundles of relationships that maintain themselves by adjusting their own behaviour in anticipation of changes to the patterns of activity all around them.

points in 3-D coordinate space, dimensions, angles and curvature radii. D'Arcy Thompson's comparison of related forms within a genus proceeds by recognising in one form a deformation of another. Forms are related if one can be deformed into another by Cartesian transformation of coordinates. Comparative analysis reveals what is missing in any singular description of a form, no matter how precise, and that is the morphogenetic tendency between forms.

At around the same time the mathematician and philosopher Whitehead[4] argued that process rather than substance was the fundamental constituent of the world, and that nature consists of patterns of activity interacting with each other. Organisms are bundles of relationships that maintain themselves by adjusting their own behaviour in anticipation of changes to the patterns of activity all around them. Anticipation and response make up the dynamic of life.

The union of these two groups of ideas is very interesting – form and behaviour emerge from process. It is process that produces, elaborates and maintains the form or structure of biological organisms (and nonbiological things), and that process consists of a complex series of exchanges between the organism and its environment. Furthermore, the organism has a capacity for maintaining its continuity and integrity by changing aspects of its behaviour. Forms are related by morphogenetic tendencies, and there is also the suggestion that some, if not all, of these characteristics are amenable to being modelled mathematically. The ideas are particularly relevant to us, as in recent years both

architecture and engineering have been preoccupied with processes for generating designs of forms in physical and computational environments.

Pattern, Behaviour and Self-Organisation

Form and behaviour have an intricate relationship. The form of an organism affects its behaviour in the environment, and a particular behaviour will produce different results in different environments, or if performed by different forms in the same environment. Behaviour is nonlinear and context specific. Mathematical descriptions of behaviour are found in the elaboration of Whitehead's 'anticipation and response' by Norbert Weiner, who developed the first systematic description of responsive behaviour in machines and animals.[5] Weiner argued that the only significant difference between controlling anti-aircraft fire and biological systems was the degree of complexity. He had developed new programs for ballistics guidance, in which information about the speed and trajectory of a target is input to a control system so that anti-aircraft guns could be aimed at the point where a target would be. The control system could record and analyse the data from a series of such experiences and subsequently modify its movements.

Cybernetics organises the mathematics of responsive behaviour into a general theory of how machines, organisms and phenomena maintain themselves over time. It uses digital and numerical processes in which pieces of information interact and the transmission of information is optimised.[6] Feedback is understood as a kind of 'steering' device that regulates behaviour, using information from the environment to measure the actual performance against a desired or optimal performance.

Work in thermodynamics by Prigogine[7] extended this (and the second law of thermodynamics) by setting up a rigorous and well-grounded study of pattern formation

each reorganisation to be produced at the moment of the collapse in the equilibrium of systems extends beyond the energy relations of an organism and its environment. Evolutionary development in general emerges from dynamic systems.[8]

Geometry and Morphogenesis

Theoreticians fiercely contest the precise relationship of morphogenesis to genetic coding, but there is an argument that it is not the form of the organism that is genetically encoded but rather the process of self-generation of the form within an environment. Geometry has a subtle role in morphogenesis. It is necessary to think of the geometry of a biological or computational form not only as the description of the fully developed form, but also as the set of boundary constraints that act as a local organising principle for self-organisation during morphogenesis. Pattern and feedback are as significant in the models of morphogenesis as they are in the models of cybernetics and dynamic systems. Alan Turing put forward a hypothesis of geometrical phyllotaxis, the development of form in plants, which offered a general theory of the morphogenesis of cylindrical lattices. These are formed locally rather than globally, node by node, and are further modified by growth. To mathematically model this process, it is necessary to have a global informing geometry, the cylinder, and a set of local rules for lattice nodes.

Turing had a lifelong interest in the morphogenesis[9] of daisies and fir cones, of polygonally symmetrical structures such as starfish, of the frequency of the appearance of the Fibonacci series in the arrangements of leaves on the stem of a plant, and of the formation of patterns such as spots or stripes. His simple early model of morphogenesis[10] demonstrates breakdown of symmetry and homogeneity, or the emergence of a pattern, in an originally homogeneous mixture of two substances. Equations describe the nonlinear changes of concentrations of two chemicals (morphogens) over time, as the chemicals react and diffuse into each other. It offers a hypothesis of the generation of pattern from a smooth sheet of cells during development in the formation of buds, skin markings and limbs. Chemicals accumulate until sufficient density is reached, then act as morphogens to generate organs.

The reaction-diffusion model is still of interest in mathematical biology, in which a great deal of research is concentrated on the interrelated dynamics of pattern and form. Turing's model operates on a single plane, or a flat sheet of cells. Some current research[11] in the computational modelling of morphogenesis extends the process that Turing outlined on flat sheets to processes in curved sheets. Geometry is inherent in these models of process, incorporating morphological 'units' that

and self-organisation that is still of use in the experimental study and theoretical analysis of biological and nonbiological systems. He argued that all biological organisms and many natural nonliving systems are maintained by the flow of energy through the system. The pattern of energy flow is subject to many small variations, which are adjusted by 'feedback' from the environment to maintain equilibrium, but occasionally there is such an amplification that the system must reorganise or collapse. A new order emerges from the chaos of the system at the point of collapse. The reorganisation creates a more complex structure, with a higher flow of energy through it, and is in turn more susceptible to fluctuations and subsequent collapse or reorganisation. The tendency of 'self-organised' systems to ever-increasing complexity, and of

Notes
1 I include computation as part of mathematics for the sufficient reason that all computation proceeds from low-level operations on 1 and 0.
2 'In an acquisitive hereditary society he stated acquisition and inheritance as the primary means of survival': Geoffrey West, *Charles Darwin: A Portrait*, Yale University Press (New Haven, CT) 1938, p 334, and 'the application of economics to biology': Oswald Spengler, *The Decline of the West*, Knopf (New York), 1939, p 373.
3 D'Arcy Thompson, *On Growth and Form*, Cambridge University Press, 1961 (first published 1917).
4 Alfred North Whitehead, *The Concept of Nature*, Cambridge University Press, 1920.
5 Norbert Weiner, *Cybernetics, or Control and Communication in the Animal and the Machine*, MIT Press (Cambridge, MA), 1961.
6 CE Shannon and W Weaver, *The Mathematical Theory of Communication*, fifth edition, University of Illinois Press (Chicago), 1963.
7 Ilya Prigogine, *Introduction to Thermodynamics of Irreversible Processes*, John Wiley (Chichester), 1967.
8 Any physical system that can be described by mathematical tools or heuristic rules is regarded as a dynamic system. Dynamic system theory classifies systems by the mathematical tool rather than the visible form of a system.
9 PT Saunders (ed), *The Collected Works of AM Turing, Volume 3, Morphogenesis*, includes 'The chemical basis of morphogenesis' (Philosophical Transactions, 1952), 'A diffusion reaction theory of morphogenesis in plants', 'Morphogen theory of phyllotaxis: geometrical and descriptive phyllotaxis', and 'Chemical theory of morphogenesis'.
10 Allen Turing, 'The chemical basis of morphogenesis', *Philosophical Transactions*, 1952.
11 Christopher J Marzek, 'Mathematical morphogenesis', Institute for Molecular Stereodynamics; 'A pragmatic approach to modelling morphogenesis', *Journal of Biological Systems*, Vol 7, 2, 1999; 'The morphogenesis of high symmetry: the symmetrisation theorem, *Journal of Biological Systems*, Vol 7, 1, 1999; 'The morphogenesis of high symmetry: the warping theorem', *Journal of Biological*

have a dynamic relationship to each other, and to an informing global geometry.

Cummings argues that the interaction and diffusion of morphogens in cellular layers[12] is also affected by the Gaussian and mean curvature of the particular membrane or layer,[13] so that changes to any particular curve in a curved membrane will produce reciprocal changes to curvature elsewhere. Successful computational models have recently extended this approach by incorporating the mathematics of curvilinear coordinate meshes used in fluid dynamics to the simulation of the morphogenesis of asymmetrical organs and limbs.[14] Folding and buckling of flat and curved sheets of cells are the basis of morphogenesis in asexual reproduction.

The lineages of organisms that reproduce asexually exhibit convergent evolution, similar forms and properties emerging without common ancestors. There are generic patterns in natural morphogenesis, and this adds to the set of geometrical operations in these mathematical models. An intricate choreography of geometrical constraints and geometrical processes is fundamental to self-organisation in biological morphogenesis. Computational models of morphogenetic processes can be adapted for architectural research, and self-organisation of material systems is evidenced in physical form-finding processes.

The Dynamics of Differentiation and Integration

Feedback is not only important for the maintenance of form in an environment; it is also a useful concept in modelling the relationship of geometrical pattern and form during biological morphogenesis. In pattern-form models, feedback is organised in two loops: from form to pattern and from pattern to form. In these models the unstructured formation of biochemical pattern causes morphogenetic 'movements' and a consequent transformation in geometry. The change in geometry disrupts the pattern and a new pattern emerges, which initiates new morphogenetic movements. The process continues until the distribution of morphogens is in equilibrium with the geometry of the evolving form in the model. The feedback loops, from pattern to form and from form to pattern, construct a mathematical model of morphogenesis[15] as a dynamic process from which form emerges.

Cybernetics, system theory and complexity have a common conceptual basis, as is evidenced by the frequency of the terms 'sciences of complexity' and 'complex adaptive systems' in the extensive literature of thermodynamics, artificial intelligence, neural networks and dynamical systems. Mathematically, too, there are commonalities in the approach to computational modelling and simulations. It is axiomatic in contemporary cybernetics that systems increase in complexity, and that in natural evolution systems emerge in increasing complexity, from cells to multicellular organisms, from humans to society and culture.

System theory argues that the concepts and principles of organisation in natural systems are independent of the domain of any one particular system, and contemporary research tends to concentrate on 'complex adaptive systems' that are self-regulating. What is common to both is the study of organisation, its structure and function. Complexity theory[16] formalises the mathematical structure of the process of systems from which complexity emerges. It focuses on the effects produced by the collective behaviour of many simple units that interact with each other, such as atoms, molecules or cells. The complex is heterogeneous, with many varied parts that have multiple connections between them, and the different parts behave differently, although they are not independent. Complexity increases when the variety (distinction) and dependency (connection) of parts increases. The process of increasing variety is called differentiation, and the process of increasing the number or the strength of connections is called integration. Evolution produces differentiation and integration in many 'scales' that interact with each other, from the formation and structure of an individual organism to species and ecosystems.

The Genetics of Collective Behaviour

The collective behaviour of semi-autonomous individual organisms is exhibited in the social or group dynamics of many natural species. Flocks of birds and schools of fish produce what appears to be an overall coherent form or array, without any leader or central directing intelligence. Insects such as bees and termites produce complex built artefacts and highly organised functional specialisations without central planning or instructions. Structured behaviour emerges from the repetition and interaction of simple rules. Mathematical models have been derived from natural phenomena, massively parallel arrays of individual 'agents', or 'cell units' that have very simple processes in each unit, with simple interactions between them. Complex patterns and effects emerge from distributed dynamical models. Wolfram's extensive study of cellular automata[17] offers a comprehensive account of their characteristics and potential. The study and simulation of co-evolution and co-adaptation is particularly effective in distributed models.

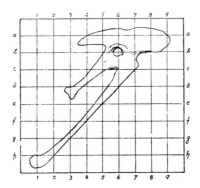

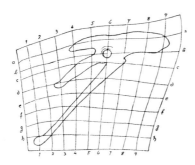

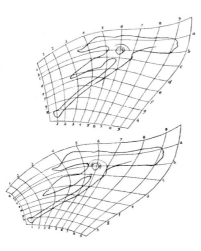

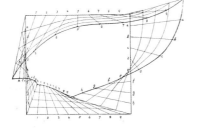

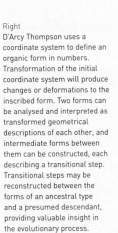

The current work at the Santa Fe Institute uses heterogeneous networks of interacting agents to pursue studies in self-organisation. The objective is to develop computational simulations of life, involving gene activity, molecular dynamics, morphogenesis and life cycles – virtual organisms with realistic morphologies that have artificial life.

Adaptive processes in natural systems provided the initiating concepts for the first genetic algorithms, developed by Holland to design artificial systems based on natural ones.[18] Genetic algorithms initiate and maintain a population of computational individuals, each of which has a genotype and a phenotype. Sexual reproduction is simulated by random selection of two individuals to provide 'parents' from which 'offspring' are produced. By using crossover (random allocation of genes from the parents' genotype) and mutation, varied offspring are generated until they fill the population. All parents are discarded, and the process is iterated for as many generations as are required to produce a population that has among it a range of suitable individuals to satisfy the fitness criteria. They are widely used today in control and optimisation applications and the modelling of ecological systems.

Mathematical simulations of genes acting in Boolean networks with varying strengths of connection can produce differentiation of tissues and organs in models, and Kauffman[19] argues that the self-organisation produced by such networks is complementary, rather than opposed, to Darwin's selection by fitness to the environment. The solution to the central problem of how to introduce the dynamics of gene processes into Cummings's model of morphogenesis is suggested by Kauffman's work on periodic attractors in genetic networks.

The concepts and mathematical techniques to produce collective behaviour from simple local responses have the potential to radically change architectural environmental systems. It is evident that the current methods of producing 'smart' buildings with hybrid mechanical systems that are controlled by a remote central computer are inferior conceptually and prone to failure in operation. The self-organising capabilities of distributed dynamic systems have produced intelligent behaviour in natural organisms and in computational simulations, and await architectural applications.

Models of self-organisation based on distributed variation and selection have been put forward by Heylighen.[20] In this argument is the view common to many approaches, in which complex systems, such as organisms and ecologies, are evolved from the interactions of elements that combine into a variety of 'assemblies'. Some 'assemblies' survive to go on to form naturally selected wholes, while others collapse to undergo further evolution. The process repeats at

Systems, Vol 7, 2, 1999.
12 LG Harrison and M Kolar, 'Coupling between reaction-diffusion and expressed morphogenesis', *Journal of Theoretical Biology*, 130, 1988, and A Hunding, SA Kauffman and BC Goodwin, 'Drosophila segmentation: supercomputer simulation of prepattern hierarchy', *Journal of Theoretical Biology*, 145, 1990.
13 FW Cummings, 'A pattern surface interactive model of morphogenesis', *Journal of Theoretical Biology*,116, 1985; 'On surface geometry coupled to morphogen', *Journal of Theoretical Biology*, 137,1989, 1990; 'A model of morphogenetic movement', *Journal of Theoretical Biology*,144,1990.
14 CH Leung and M Berzins, *A Computational Model for Organism Growth Based on Surface Mesh Generation*, University of Leeds, 2002.
15 Alexander V Spirirov, 'The change in initial symmetry in the pattern-form interaction model of sea urchin gastrulation, *Journal of Theoretical Biology*, 161, 1993.
16 Warren Weaver, 'Science and complexity', *American Scientist*, 36, 536, 1948.
17 Stephen Wolfram, *A New Kind of Science*, Wolfram Media (Illinois), 2002, and *Cellular Automata and Complexity: Collected Papers*, Addison-Wesley (Reading, MA), 1994.
18 John H Holland, *Adaptation in Natural and Artificial Systems: An Introductory Analysis with Applications to Biology, Control and Artificial Intelligence*, MIT Press (Cambridge, MA), 1992 (first published 1975), and *Hidden Order: How Adaptation Builds Complexity*, Addison-Wesley (Reading, MA), 1996.
19 SA Kauffman, 'Antichaos and adaptation', *Scientific American*, August 1991; *The Origins of Order: Self-Organisation and Selection in Evolution*, Oxford University Press, 1993; *At Home in the Universe: The Search for Laws of Self-Organisation and Complexity*, Oxford University Press, 1995.
20 Francis Heylighen, 'Self-Organisation, Emergence and the Architecture of Complexity', *Proceedings of 1st European Conference on System Science*, 1989.
21 HA Simon, 'The Architecture of Complexity', *Proceedings of the American Philosophical Society* 106, reprinted in *The Sciences of the Artificial*, third edition, MIT Press (Cambridge, MA), 1996.
22 I Stewart, 'Self-organisation in evolution: a mathematical perspective', *Philosophical Transactions*, The Royal Society of London, 361, 2003.

higher levels, an emergent whole at one level becoming a component of a system emerging at a higher level.[21] Further, natural evolution is in general not a single system but distributed or parallel, with multiple systems co-evolving with partial autonomy and some interaction. Self-organisation of the ecology as a whole is as critical as the morphogenetic self-organisation of an individual within it.

A very recent series of models have been developed based on phenotypes rather than genotypes or genetic activity.[22] Stewart argues that all self-organising systems are organised not just by themselves, but also by their contexts. The focus in this approach to modelling evolutionary self-organisation is on speciation, fitness landscapes and species selection. The models exhibit nonlinear and collective effects and represent speciation as a symmetry-breaking bifurcation. They are collections of ordinary differential equations arranged in network structures, and the network topology is reflected in the form of the equations. Recombination is preferred to mutation, as it produces substantial diversity in each generation, and selection operates on individual organisms in the context of other organisms and the environment.

Architecture and Emergence

In answer to the question: What is it that emerges, what does it emerge from, and how is emergence produced? we can say the following.

Form and behaviour emerge from the processes of complex systems. Processes produce, elaborate and maintain the form of natural systems, and those processes include dynamic exchanges with the environment. There are generic patterns in the process of self-generation of forms, and in forms themselves. Geometry has both a local and a global role in the interrelated dynamics of pattern and form in self-organised morphogenesis.

Forms maintain their continuity and integrity by changing aspects of their behaviour and by their iteration over many generations. Forms exist in varied populations, and where communication between forms is effective, collective structured behaviour and intelligence emerges.

The systems from which form emerges, and the systems within individual complex forms themselves, are maintained by the flow of energy and information through the system. The pattern of flow has constant variations, adjusted to maintain equilibrium by 'feedback' from the environment. Natural evolution is not

a single system but distributed, with multiple systems co-evolving in partial autonomy and with some interaction. An emergent whole form can be a component of a system emerging at a higher level – and what is 'system' for one process can be 'environment' for another.

Emergence is of momentous importance to architecture, demanding substantial revisions to the way in which we produce designs. We can use the mathematical models outlined above for generating designs, evolving forms and structures in morphogenetic processes within computational environments. Criteria for selection of the 'fittest' can be developed that correspond to architectural requirements of performance, including structural integrity and 'buildability'. Strategies for design are not truly evolutionary unless they include iterations of physical (phenotypic) modelling, incorporating the self-organising material effects of form finding and the industrial logic of production available in CNC and laser-cutting modelling machines.

The logic of emergence demands that we recognise that buildings have a life span, sometimes of many decades, and that throughout that life they have to maintain complex energy and material systems. At the end of their life span they must be dissembled and the physical materials recycled. The environmental performance of buildings must also be rethought. The current hybrid mechanical systems with remote central processors limit the potential achievement of 'smart' buildings. Intelligent environmental behaviour of individual buildings and other artefacts can be much more effectively produced and maintained by the collective behaviour of distributed systems.

We must extend this thinking beyond the response of any single individual building to its environment. Each building is part of the environment of its neighbours, and it follows that 'urban' environmental intelligence can be achieved by the extension of data communication between the environmental systems of neighbouring buildings. Urban transport infrastructure must be organised to have similar environmental responsive systems, not only to control internal environments of stations and subways, but also to manage the response to the fluctuating discharge of people onto streets and into buildings. Linking the response of infrastructure systems to groups of environmentally intelligent buildings will allow higher-level behaviour to emerge.

We are within the horizon of a systemic change, from the design and production of individual 'signature' buildings to an ecology in which evolutionary designs have sufficient intelligence to adapt and to communicate, and from which intelligent cities will emerge. ∆

Frei

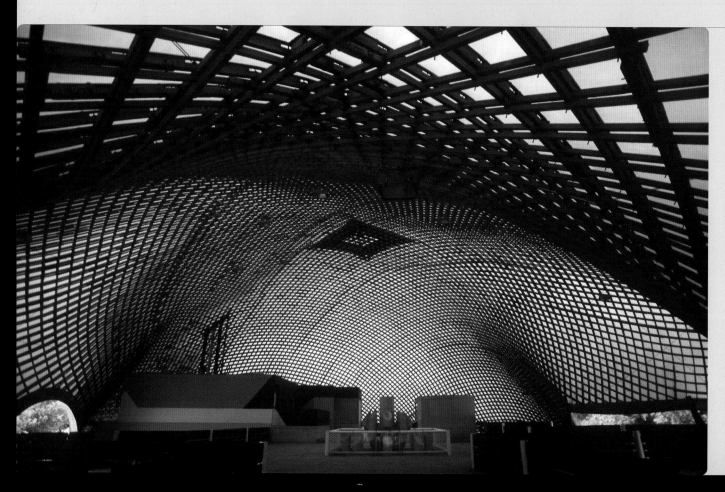

Otto

In Conversation with the Emergence and Design Group

Frei Otto has been an architect for five decades, and his pioneering work is noted for construction innovations in many materials and building forms. Here, in conversation with the **Emergence and Design Group**, he discusses the development of form-finding techniques. This is one significant aspect of his interest in natural systems, in the relation of experimental models to geometry andin iterative mathematics. He concludes with a commentary on the contribution of irregularity to the strength in biological and architectural structures, and the proposal that to understand living nature is an important task for the future.

'A technician observing living nature just cannot grasp living objects which die so quickly, are so sensitive, so complex and both so unimitable and strange. A biologist looking on technology sees how imperfect technical activity is. Both recognise today that technical and biological objects will never be the only optima which can be thought of, but only short-term stations in a flow of unique biological-technical developments without a recognisable target.'[1]

Frei Otto's innovative and prolific research includes a broad range of studies in nature as a source for architectural and engineering design, and is always directed towards applications in construction. The following conversation focuses on only a few aspects of Frei Otto's enormous body of work: on issues of modelling through form finding, on future developments of this kind of research and future tasks for the discipline of architecture.

Frei Otto is particularly interested in the natural processes of self-generation of forms, and in the structural behaviour of those forms. This led him to develop novel physical form-finding experiments, the first architect since Gaudí to do so. The scope of his investigations includes experiments for producing pressure-loaded vault forms by reversing tension-loaded suspended forms, soap-film experiments for producing minimal surfaces, and experiments for the investigation of optimised path systems and branched constructions.

In his work, form finding is a design instrument, based on empirical processes that utilise the self-organisation of material systems under the influence of extrinsic forces. The range of possible forms is determined by the choice and definition of the conditions under which the form-finding process takes place.

Uniting the logic of material and of structure makes it possible to form-find certain kinds of structures at all stages, from the beginning of the design process to full-scale construction. We asked Frei Otto how he became interested in nature as a source for the principles of his form-finding experiments.

'In 1960 I was at the Technical University of Berlin as an instructor, and I had given a seminar on lightweight architecture, when I learnt that the leading biologist and anthropologist Johann-Gerhard Helmcke was interested in the works of Konrad Wachsman, Buckminster Fuller and Nervi and was also quite well informed about my work. We met and talked, and within the same year we founded a research group called "Biology and Building". We have collaborated since then.

'I have always worked strictly as an architect in collaboration, although I have tried to understand the form-making processes in biology. Nevertheless, my first experiments were not related to biology. I was interested in the form-making processes in nonliving nature, such as how clouds or sand waves are formed. It was obvious to me that these processes can be directly used for building. I have been very interested in hanging structures since 1951. The mathematics of hanging structures is complicated and so I tried to model these structures directly. I started with tents and cable nets. When you are hanging a chain you can use its shape for a roof. The single catenary line in mathematics is not simple, but it is so easy to turn your drawing board to a vertical plane and hang a chain in front of it and you have the line. It is simple, and you see that it must be a correct shape for a structure because if you touch the chain it always goes back to exactly the same position. It is a way to demonstrate the structural correctness of the design without mathematics.

'From a single chain, I then went to work with a net of chains, and from there I moved to the minimal surface. A minimal surface can be made very exactly with soap film. The film is flexible, but you will only find one minimal surface for a given frame. I started looking into these self-organising processes that I could use in my architecture. Mathematical formulae for many minimal surfaces found in physical processes have yet to be determined. In most cases you measure your model and define the surface so exactly that it can be built. There is no material from which a full-scale minimal surface can be built, so you have to use a mesh, woven materials or cable nets, and the difference between the surface of a cable net and a minimal surface is not big. A tensioned skin always wants to go in the direction of a minimal surface, and every load on a materialised minimal surface changes it, so you then have another surface that is thicker and that is stressed. I am not saying that one must use a minimal surface, but it is very good to know about it.'

Opening page
Frei Otto, Multihalle
Mannheim, Germany, 1975.

Below
The Frei Otto–Maeda Workshop 2003 took place at Hooke Park, Dorset, UK, in the workshop facilities of the Architectural Association School of Architecture, which were partly designed by Frei Otto. During the workshop, various form-finding experiments were conducted and analysed, including compressive-stressed inverted forms, minimal surfaces, moving pneus and aggregates.

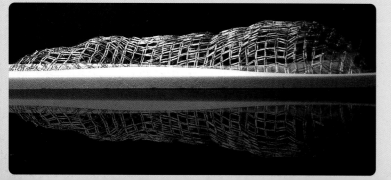

Multihalle Mannheim

Grid shells resist loads through 3-D curvature, which significantly increases the capacity of shells to resist concentrated loading and reduces the tendency to buckle out of plane. The form of grid shells can be established through form-finding methods, which deploy the physical process of self-organisation of a material system under the influence of extrinsic forces. The range of possible forms is determined by the choice of the conditions under which the process takes place.

The Multihalle in Mannheim in Germany was the first built grid-shell, and the design was developed through a series of form-finding models. Once the overall form was satisfactory, a detailed nonrigid suspended net model was built. A nonrigid net assumes, under its own weight, a spatially curved suspended form with only tensile forces acting on it. The inverted form is called a thrust surface, which is free of moments and stressed by axial compression. The conversion of the form of the suspended net model is the basis for the construction of a grid shell.

The suspended model was measured photogrammetrically at the Institute for Applied Geodesy in Buildings at the University of Stuttgart, under the direction of Klaus Linkwitz, a long-time collaborator of Frei Otto. From the measuring results, the coordinates of the knot points were calculated from the reversed to the real measurements of the enlarged model. After the final calculations were completed it was found that a double-layered grid with special sliding connections would be required. Diagonal cables were added to keep bending deformations within limits and to guarantee stability.

During the construction the timber laths, which were laid out flat, were lifted into shape and then fixed at the boundaries and the node bolts tightened. A physical load test was carried out on part of the grid shell, and water-filled municipal dustbins were hung from every ninth node. Double-exposure photography was used to record the deflection. The actual deflection caused by the physical load test was much less than that calculated by computer.

Form and force are correlated, in that the form of a structure can be determined as the state in which the forces acting in and on it are in equilibrium. Furthermore, the flow of force can be shown through physical modelling. Frei Otto has developed many different methods of experimental modelling, using principles of the self-organisation of materials into lightweight, stable configurations.

The characteristics and behaviour of a form that has been evolved from a self-forming process have to be physically tested in experiments. Self-forming processes can be systematised by two distinct approaches. The first system emphasises the force, which acts in a structure or can be transmitted by it, or which was active during its development. The second system emphasises the form of the developing object because its form is a primary parameter in the evaluation of a structure. Form and force are correlated, in that the form of a structure can be determined as the state in which the forces acting in and on it are in equilibrium. Furthermore, the flow of force can be shown through physical modelling. Frei Otto has developed many different methods of experimental modelling, using principles of the self-organisation of materials into lightweight, stable configurations. We asked him to elaborate on the relationship between geometry, materials and models, and to describe how he started his work at the Institute of Lightweight Structures.

'About 5,000 years ago knowledge of geometry started to be used in building, making straight lines with a stretched thread, using the right angle in

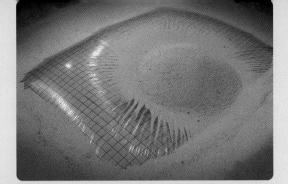

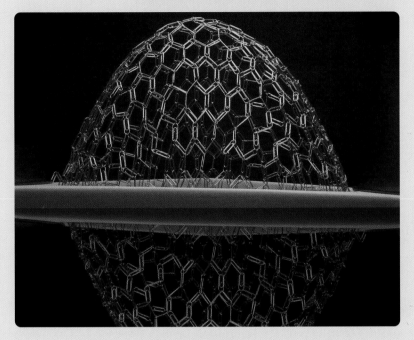

institute at the University of Stuttgart to explore these modelling methods. Leonhardt built suspension bridges and high towers at a time when the mathematical proofs of structural stability were quite limited. He started modelling himself, measuring deformation and then comparing those measurements with his calculations. I worked with him on several large projects, including the Bremen Harbour Roof and the German Pavilion in Montreal. In Cologne we had to span an arch stabilised with a glass-fibre membrane. It was the combination of structural calculation and modelling together that succeeded. A correctly made model does prove a structure. It is difficult to know if a theoretically determined shape is structurally stable until it is built. For example, it is beneficial to prove through a model the stability of a thin shell structure which is often very weak against buckling.'

While Frei Otto has greatly advanced the field of form finding through physical modelling, he has also been involved with the development of digital form finding and analysis. In fact, most constructions built by Frei Otto after 1970 were computer generated and computer drawn. Upon his suggestion computer simulation was introduced by the geodesic expert Klaus Linkwitz in 1966. Frei Otto also collaborated with John H Argyris, the inventor of 'finite elements'. While today it is possible to use scanning or digitising technology to transfer from a physical model to a digital model, and from this produce drawings, we wondered how Frei Otto during the past decades developed techniques to transfer data from physical models to drawings and subsequently to computational models.

'In the early days, when I had little money and worked by myself, I had to work with photographs and a measuring table that I developed myself. With this set-up I could draw contours that were exact to the tenth of a millimetre. Later I worked with the geodesic expert Klaus Linkwitz, and we used the stereoscopic method that is used for measuring the surface of the earth. Interestingly, at the same time the biologist Johann-Gerhard Helmcke was testing stereoscopic measurements with electron microscopes. His specialist field was very small living objects, diatomes and radioloria. Helmcke collaborated with Konrad Zuse, who invented the computer and used it in combination with the stereo-comparator for the photogrammetry. We used this method on models for the German Pavilion in Montreal. We also put Konrad Zuse's computer in the World Exposition, together with a computer-controlled drawing machine, plotting the sections of our building.

'We have used the computer ever since then, but I continue to use models as well. Our models, in combination with iterative calculations, have really helped us to make better and more beautiful buildings. I am not against digital processes at all, but emphasise

horizontal and vertical directions. These geometries were considered as an optimum for structures. This allowed building masters to make buildings very directly. The Egyptians and the Romans knew that the sphere and the cylinder are not always the best for structures. If you want to make a vaulted dome out of stone you may discover that the conical shape is better than a hemisphere. With modelling I could come very near to the optimum. With models I do not have to use simple geometries, and forms and shapes can be developed and tested for stability against the forces in nature: earthquakes, winds or snow. Most of the mathematics of minimum surface structures are complicated or unknown, so that it is much faster for me to find the form. In five seconds one can make a minimal surface that would take months to describe and to prove structurally stable.

'Today I use many different modelling methods, perhaps as many as 200. In the 1960s Fritz Leonhardt, one of Germany's greatest engineers, asked me to found a research

Above
Examples from the
Frei Otto-Maeda
Workshop 2003.

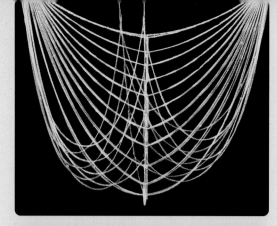

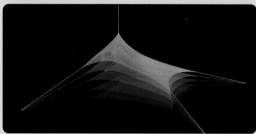

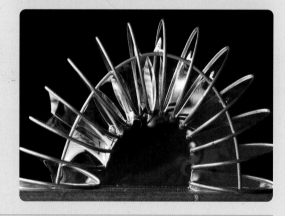

Right
Examples from the
Frei Otto-Maeda
Workshop 2003.

'Finding the first shapes and understanding the structure is best done with small inexpensive models, some of which can be built in a few hours. If the form is new, then there will be no mathematical precedent and calculations are not immediately possible and models must be used. However, modelling is only a small part of the total job that an architect has to do in order to arrive at a building design, especially if the building has a complex function.'

the importance of understanding of what we are doing. Solving problems with software programs that are not specially written for the particular problem one is dealing with may lead to a lack of understanding of what is shown on the screen. Something may look perfect on the monitor, but that does not mean that you understand it or that it is functioning in real size.

'In 1967/68 I began to collaborate with Ove Arup. He asked me to develop a modelling shop for him, which I led for three years until Ted Happold left Arup and moved to Bath. Arup, Happold and Leonhardt, the best engineers in the world at that time, all used a combined technique of modelling and iterative mathematics. I think this is the key to the future. In physics, for example, it is understood that a new formula is only proved when confirmed by experiment. Even Einstein confirmed his formulae by experiment. You can prove the stability of a building in the actual building itself, as we did with the finished structure of the German Pavilion. We used a hydraulic jack and measured the forces in all masts and cables for the whole pavilion, but this was an exception. We could have built it only with modelling and measuring, and without mathematical proof.

'For testing forces the model must be made with the same materials and in the same form as the final structure. You can do this with steel wires, but it is nearly impossible with concrete. If the materials and the form are exactly the same as the final building, and if the model has the same load per square metre, then the same stresses appear in the model as in the building. It is not always necessary to make every model like this, but it is important to start with simple models to test the feasibility of the design. Obviously, models for detailed analysis take longer to make and are more expensive. Finding the first shapes and understanding the structure is best done with small inexpensive models, some of which can be built in a few hours. If the form is new, then there will be no mathematical precedent and calculations are not immediately possible and models must be used. However, modelling is only a small part of the total job that an architect has to do in order to arrive at a building design, especially if the building has a complex function.'

Frei Otto's immense body of work contains many indications of exciting directions for further research and developments. We asked Frei Otto to reflect on his personal view of the primary tasks that architecture needs to take on in the near future, as well as further interesting areas of research.

'We need a worldwide technical organisation and new inventions to improve our buildings so that they can survive catastrophes. We need a system that allows us to react quickly, with appropriate ships, aircraft, helicopters, and we need instant buildings for those people who are affected by catastrophes. Earthquakes require the solving of special technical problems. There are some quite good technical solutions but knowledge

Above
Multihalle Mannheim.

Notes
1 Frei Otto, 'Zum Vorbild
Natur', in *Morphology/
Neobiology, Form+Zweck*
17, Form+Zweck Verlag
(Berlin), 2000.
2 For a comprehensive
summary of Frei Otto's
experiments refer to: Frei
Otto and Bodo Rasch, *Finding
Form*, Edition Axel Menges
(Germany), 1995. For more
detailed elaborations refer
to *IL 25 Experiments – Form-
Force-Mass 5*, Institute of
Lightweight Structures,
University of Stuttgart, 1990.
For references on specific
modelling and form-finding
topics refer to the publication
series of the Institute of
Lightweight Structures at
the University of Stuttgart.

of them is not widely distributed. Some architects and engineers say that buildings made from brick or stone are too weak for earthquake regions, but they can perform well if they have the correct shape to resist earthquake forces. We have to study the reasons for this, because most of the knowledge of earthquake-resistant design in the past is lost. I have tried to experiment with stones and inclining models, which is the easiest and most revealing way to test stability.

'We have also studied the "domino effect" caused by tearing in skyscrapers. The reason for the collapse of the World Trade Center was the domino effect. We studied the collapse of the building with our English friends. In biological structures the transmission of forces takes place mostly through the skin. Biological evolution began with nonstiff structures.

The stiff structures came much later, and they are usually just stiffening parts of larger soft structures. We need to study biological structures much more. They have usually only one structural element, a skin filled with water, proliferated in an infinite variety of ways. The skin is made out of fibres, a thin net. Fibres are the secret to understanding biological structures, and they don't tear. You cannot tear a living skin, but you can tear a well-woven cloth. Living structure is completely different to artificial technical structures that are shaped by simple geometries. The structure of living nature is very complex. In living structure every element is different. This is why living structures do not tear easily. Irregularity is important not only in biology but also in technology, and is a field that has not been researched enough.

'It is necessary that we architects try to understand living nature, but not to copy it. This is one very important task for the future.'[2] △D

Finding Exotic Form: An Evolution of Form Finding as a Design Method

Michael Hensel, of OCEAN NORTH, argues the need for an alternative form-finding technique that can incorporate dynamics and extend the form-finding process beyond construction to in situ form adaptation. He presents his case for an expanded form-finding tool-set in relation to a design study for the World Center for Human Concerns, which is based on the notion of 'parasite buildings' that are wrapped around existing buildings. In this case the required structural and circulatory independence from the host building is resolved by the building skin of the wrapped structure.

'Nothing retains its own form'
— Pythagoras

Opposite, top
View of the World Center in the context of Lower Manhattan.

Opposite, bottom
Close-up of the building envelope and the vertical circulation channels

Right, top
View of the World Center from West Broadway.

Right, bottom
View of the World Center from the junction of 12th Avenue and Canal Street.

Material Dynamic: Form Adaptation and Feedback

Form finding is a design method that deploys and instrumentalises the self-organisation of material systems under the influence of extrinsic forces. In architectural design and engineering, form finding is commonly used to develop structural form in response to gravity. Its two primary tasks are the generation of the form to be built and the full-scale construction of the desired form. These co-joined tasks lead to finite building solutions. This essay proposes that finite designs resulting from form-finding processes are at odds with understanding material systems as inherently dynamic. This understanding necessitates a dramatic shift in focus of the aim of architectural design from producing static and discrete objects to the generation of motile material arrangements that are responsive to their environment. The question is then: How can we approach form finding if material form continuously transmutes in response to an equally dynamic force-context?

An approach to this design problem must engage with three generative feedback processes. The first feedback concerns the

27

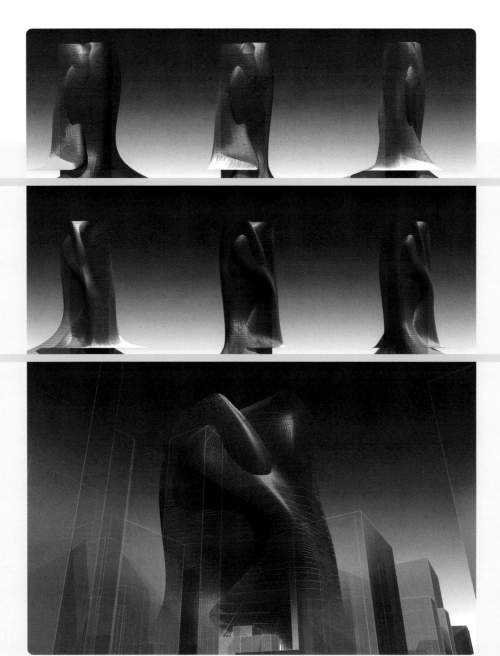

Top: Form Generation

Form generation does not necessarily need to be based on evolutionary software. Readily available animation software can be used to set into motion a formative process influenced by attracting and repelling forces. Each frame of such an animation is a Gestalt snapshot of the formative process of an object. The initial form generation of the World Center commenced by employing an animation technique that wraps surfaces around given objects. The animation consisted of 500 frames that were subsequently assessed in relation to the overall geometry of the composite object and the sectional pockets that result from the intersecting surfaces.

Middle: Geometric Analysis

Geometric analysis is of central importance for form-finding processes in a digital environment. Current 3-D-modelling software packages offer a variety of tools for geometric surface analysis. The Zebra analysis in Rhino, for example, uses NURBS surface evaluation and rendering techniques to aid visual analysis of surface smoothness, curvature, continuity between surfaces, and so on. The analysis of surface continuity helps to assess the structural consequences of how surfaces meet. Zebra analysis plots zebra stripes over a model as if it were chromium-plated and placed inside a striped cylinder. This method was developed in the car industry to help search car surfaces for bumps, folds and other deformations. Zebra analysis can highlight three types of surface continuities. If surfaces that meet edge to edge show disjointed stripes along the seam it indicates that the surfaces touch, but have a kink or crease, which implies G0 or position-only continuity between the surfaces. If the stripes show kinks or turn sharply as they cross the seam, it follows that the position and tangency between the surfaces matches. This indicates G1, or position and tangency, continuity between the surfaces. G2 surfaces, which are tangency and curvature continuous, show stripes flowing smoothly across the seam. One problem with Zebra surface analysis is that with changes of the view angle to the model, the stripe patterns change and so it can be rather difficult to analyse blends from several different angles. The Zebra analysis of the two intersecting surfaces that make up the envelope of the World Center reveal all three types of surface continuities. The result can yield two responses – either lower-degree surface continuity is eradicated by means of rebuilding the geometry of the digital 3-D model or a differentiated approach to construction is chosen in relation to local surface continuity.

Bottom: Rapid Modelling

Rapid physical output of digital models serves to comprehend complex form and to develop criteria for further assessment and development. The various technologies of rapid prototyping serve this goal particularly well, as the geometry of the digital model is correctly and swiftly manifested. Two rapid prototype models were produced as form studies for the Max Protetch exhibition 'A New World Trade Center'. The aim was to produce rapid prototype models that don't break easily in transport, as the exhibition travelled, and to use a material that is not affected by exposure to daylight. Both requirements are not easily met by a number of rapid prototyping technologies. Selective laser sintering (SLS) was chosen as the first part of the process. SLS implies parts that are built with successive layers of powder selectively bound by a laser beam. The basic material consists of powder with particle sizes in the order of magnitude of 50 micrometres. Successive powder layers are spread on top of each other. After deposition, a computer-controlled CO_2 laser beam scans the surface and selectively binds together the powder particles of the corresponding cross section of the digital model. During laser exposure the powder temperature rises above the glass transition point after which adjacent particles flow together. This process is called sintering. As polymer powder-based models remain fragile and turn yellow due to UV-light exposure, another material approach was needed. The final choice came from rapid tooling. A mix of rapid steel metal and polymer powder was sintered. The resulting steel particles were bound with polymer. The polymer was then removed by placing the initial model in a furnace. The baking process caused the polymer binders to be burnt away and resulted in a very brittle steel skeleton that was then simultaneously sintered and infiltrated with bronze, giving a highly durable model.

context-specific forces that act upon material form, which are in turn influenced by material form through levels of resistance to change. The second feedback comprises the dynamic relation between material arrangement and human subject. The third feedback involves the interactions between human subject and environment that assert indirect influence on material arrangements.[1]

To account for these processes and their combined impact in a systematic fashion it is necessary to establish a taxonomy of force-formation processes. Moreover, the underlying conceptual and methodological framework necessitates a tool-set that sets into motion formative processes and analyses emerging forms as transition-states together with their particular performative capacities. Such a tool-set needs, then, to be able to detect the performance potential of material systems in addition to the specified ones, and change its analysis and assessment criteria accordingly. The tool-set has to evolve its generative and analytical logic in parallel with the continual self-organisation of material form.

The complex dynamic interrelation between material form and environment requires a multiple control parameter set-up. Traditionally, form-finding methods focus mainly on mono-parametric structural behaviour of material form. This constitutes one-way causal relations, far from the feedback set-up required to evolve form and tool-set together. Multiple-parameter experiments involving many formative forces acting together are a fairly new undertaking, particularly when the assessment criteria incorporate such diverse items as spatial, structural, material and habitational characteristics. This becomes further complicated by the fact that the variables and the assessment criteria of a multiple-parameter form-finding experiment do not necessarily coincide. One example would be a structural form-finding experiment that yields a desirable spatial organisation that was not anticipated.

A crucial aspect in multiple-parameter experiments is the redefinition of the notion of efficiency. For instance, if only one structural parameter needs to be considered, for example in Gaudí's hanging models, the performance of the model can be optimised to a specific force-case. With multiple-parameter set-ups each result is a negotiation towards a best-possible overall performance, with a great deal of overall redundancy (future potential) built into the material arrangement so that shifts from one

force-scenario to another can be accommodated. However, negotiated performance criteria in multiple-parameter form-finding processes do not necessarily lead to mean average solutions: rather specific performance profiles may emerge in relation to the specific set of influences that yields a particular material form. The difference between the best-possible overall solution on the one hand and the mean average on the other is defined by the ability of the former to shift priorities between control parameters or even to involve new parameters on the basis of recognising opportunities in transitory states.

Form-in-transition must be able to perform in all relevant ways at all times, and not switch from one steady state to another. Dynamic form evolves through morphogenesis under changing force-cases, including both generation and adaptation of form. Adaptation of material systems in situ therefore engages a third task for form finding that commences after the construction process and proceeds by means of analysis and feedback of the impact of inhabitants and habitat onto the built environment.

Form-finding processes extend in this way beyond the design and construction phases towards a process of adaptation of the built environment. This closes the operational feedback loop. It is an inclusive process that extends the understanding of the built environment from a scaled-up version of modelled, anticipated and finite performance profiles – a hard deterministic approach – to an understanding of a mutable environment that is subjected to contingent influences. A new, soft regulatory approach must enable changes between anticipated and actual performances and assessment criteria. This suggests a design environment in which the generated is always to some extent different from the anticipated, and in which the unfamiliar appearance and behaviour of transitory states becomes the focus of interest.

Here the notion of the exotic comes into play. It refers to the unfamiliarity of shifts in patterns of appearance and behaviour, the capricious and divergent actualisation of transitory states. The condition of all states being transitory constitutes the strange and bizarre qualities of the formative processes that yield unfamiliar forms and performances. In design disciplines this is a disturbing thought. Isn't design supposed to lead to a result that can be clearly anticipated, to products that are solid, controlled and built to last? Of what use is a result that is fluid, contingent and built to change? What is the task of form finding if its result cannot be anticipated?

From a traditional viewpoint this approach turns counter to any 'rigorous' experiment by allowing for contingency and divergence and not eliminating undesired influences. Indeed this approach seems to contradict the very notion of instrumentality if the

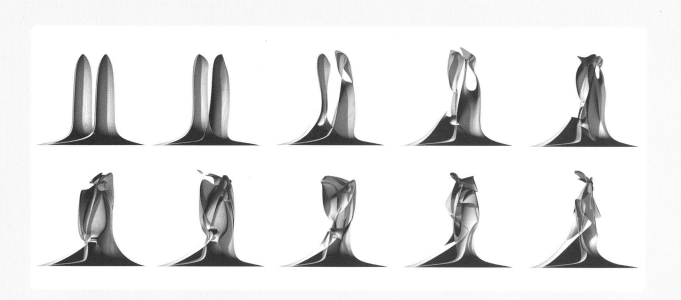

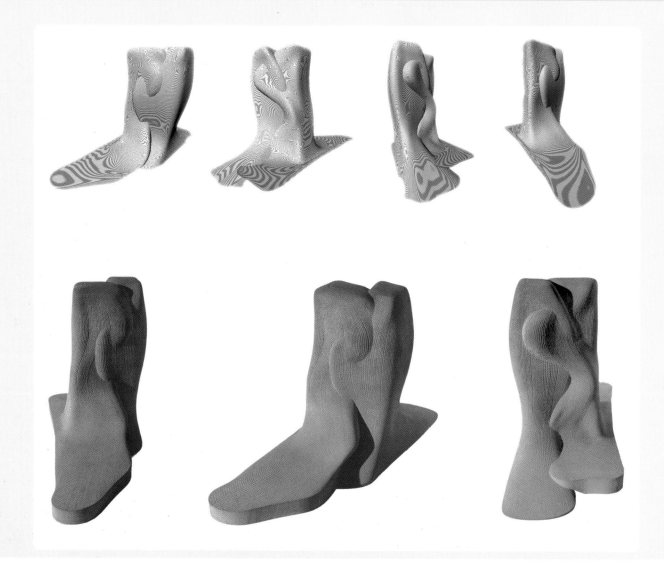

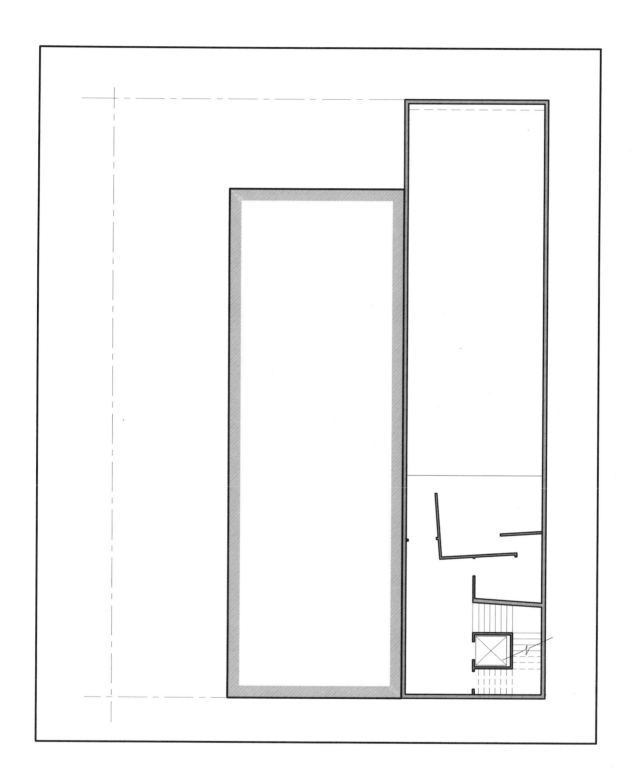

chosen set of control parameters is not strictly limited and set out in a closed system. What is interesting here is the implied reversal of experimental procedure. Common form-finding processes are based on a finite, a priori formulation of desired performance profiles for which the appropriate form is 'found'. The new approach commences from a temporal and nonfinite definition of control parameters and performance ranges, in which each transition state may bring a shift in assessment criteria that is not absolute but relative to potentials.

This implies that both the analysis and the regulation of processes that generate evolving form and performative capacity need to be based on pattern recognition, the operation and design of systems that recognise pattern in data. Moreover, inference, search or learning, which are central to artificial intelligence, are needed for advanced form finding of dynamic material form. For such a form-finding tool-set to evolve criteria for analysis and assessment alongside material form, an inductive process needs to take place that extends pattern recognition into the time dimension. Not only static pattern or form needs to be recognised, but also morphogenetic or formation pattern in relation to time- and context-specific influences.

The role of this tool-set would be to derive general rules and criteria from the observed particular circumstances, while at the same time checking these criteria against the previous ones. Such tools require an open-source structure that allows data not included in the initial control-parameter set to influence the generative feedback process. Evolutionary form-generation software usually incorporates an environment-specific random factor as well as genome mutation that, together, constitute sources of contingent influence. Indeed we are at the threshold of having multiparametric digital tools that generate and analyse combined geometric, structural, material, spatial and habitational characteristics and capacities. In combination with computer-aided manufacturing tools, such as rapid prototyping, physical models of selected transition states can be produced and tested in actual or simulated environments and the test data can be fed back into the generative process in the digital environment. An inclusive generative feedback-based and evolving tool would therefore constitute the next major step in the evolution of form-finding methods.

The conceptual and methodological framework of inclusive form-finding methods is currently being developed by the Emergent

Technologies and Design Programme and in Diploma Unit 4 at the Architectural Association, the Emergence and Design Group and OCEAN NORTH. The Emergent Technologies and Design Programme is tackling the combination of the methodological and tool-based generative set-up by using form-finding methods along with evolutionary software, as well as advanced digital 3-D modelling and computer-aided manufacturing. Diploma Unit 4 is developing an approach that integrates ecological, morphological and topological concepts and methods into a systematic pursuit of performativity and its feedback on design criteria and output. The Emergence and Design Group has worked on the development and deployment of evolutionary strategies for design with inclusive micro- and macrostructural systems.

Versatile Morphologies: Baskets and Pockets

OCEAN NORTH's research into the instrumental deployment of available CAD/CAM technology as time-based notation and design tools commenced with the Synthetic Landscape project[2] and as form-finding tools with the adrift Time Capsule entry to the New York Times Millennium Time Capsule competition.[3] The study for the World Center for Human Concerns continued this research. The Max Protetch Gallery in New York commissioned the study for the 'A New World Trade Center' exhibition in 2001 and the project has since continued as research into new approaches to high-rise parasite structures that are wrapped around existing buildings. OCEAN NORTH's scheme articulates an unfamiliar morphology that, in being alien and exotic, is able to yield unexpected relations between habitants and habitat that could in doing so result in new social arrangements.

The formal and spatial articulation of the scheme was developed through a digital form-finding process, using animation software that drapes surfaces around defined objects. The 440-metre-tall volume of the World Center was thus draped around the volume of Minoru Yamasaki's Twin Towers, which are visible as vague figures behind the textured and folded skin. This design serves to resolve the required structural independence of the parasite building from the host building, which was obviously not designed to receive additional loads or dramatically increased circulation. The spatial, structural and circulatory organisation of the World Center is thus achieved by the articulation of the building envelope. The envelope is organised as two large interlocking basket structures that are able to absorb a much higher degree of local structural disruption without collapsing than can standard central-core structures. The greater potential of the envelope to flex and to redistribute forces across the strands of the basket is given by the redundancy of structural members in basket-type morphologies.

Opposite
Sectional analysis, analysis of surface continuity and rapid modelling.

Below
A larger SLS-rapid prototype model was made for the 'Contours – Evolutionary Strategies for Design' exhibition at the Architectural Association in February 2003. The rapid prototype model served to show in a more detailed fashion the two intersecting surfaces that make up the form of the World Center.

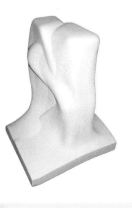

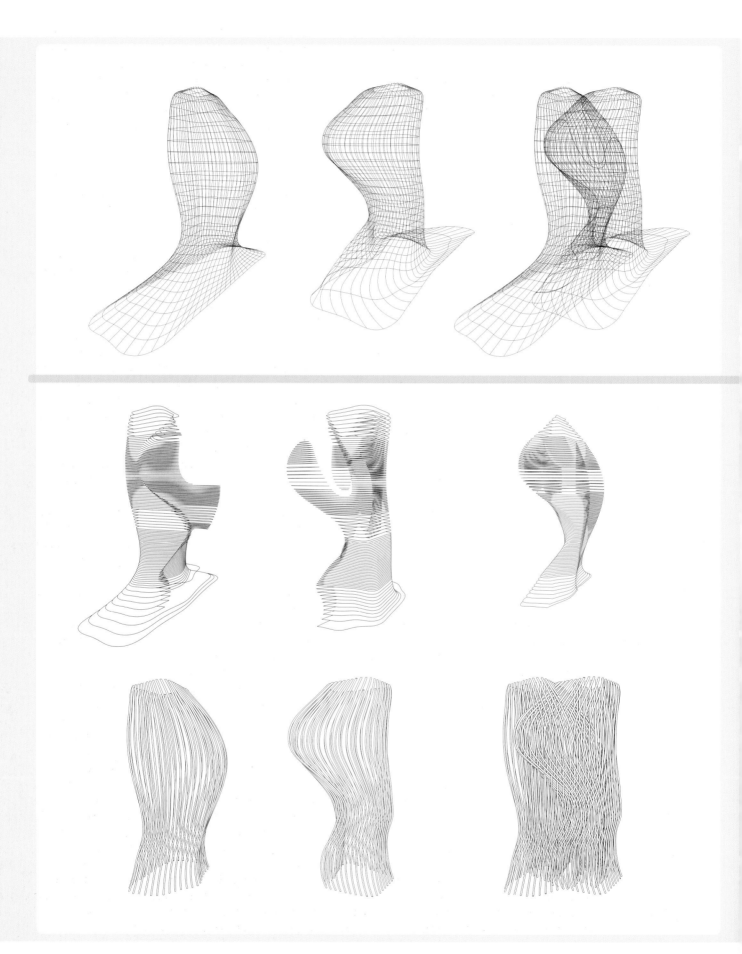

Notes
1 This aspect relates in an
interesting way to current
research in evolutionary
biology that states that
evolution does not only take
place through natural
selection, but also in so-called
niche construction. Niche
construction refers to the
process by which organisms
actively change their
environment and in
consequence create
evolutionary pressure on the
further development of the
species. This consequence is
referred to as ecological
inheritance, which does not
depend on the presence of
biological replicators but only
on the persistence of physical
changes made by ancestral
organisms in the environments
of their descendants. This
process is very apparent in the
man-made environment, with
its impact on local and global
ecosystems. For further
reference see: Kevin Laland,
Hohn Odling-Smee and Marcus
Feldman, *Niche Construction:
The Neglected Process in
Evolution*, Princeton University
Press, 2003.
2 See Johan Bettum and
Michael Hensel, 'Channelling
systems – dynamic processes
and digital time-based
methods in urban design',
*D Contemporary Processes
in Architecture*, London, 2000,
pp 36–43.
3 See Michael Hensel and Kivi
Sotamaa, 'Vigorous
environments', *D Contemporary
Techniques in Architecture*,
London, 2002, pp 34–41.

The initial form-finding criteria for the World Center were volumetric with respect to the overall building geometry and spatial with respect to the sectional articulation of the scheme as a series of interstitial spaces formed by the draped skin. These interstices are understood as urban spaces in vertical arrangement that can be individually designed and programmed by independent but coordinated design teams. This approach shifts the emphasis from the horizontal 'block' arrangements and ground-datum zoning to deep spatial planning with an increased emphasis on topological relations between three-dimensionally arranged spatial 'pockets'.

The permeability of the threshold between these pockets, or, in other words, the connectivity, becomes a qualitative criterion for the relation between the spatial pockets and circulation across the entire volume of the scheme. The scheme therefore abandons the common high-rise organisation of central service and circulation cores and uses instead the building envelope as a space for circulation: 120 vertical circulation channels are nested within the skin, and tie as reinforcement into the basket structure. This approach results in an infinite number of ways of getting around the building and facilitating social encounters en route. In doing so, the draping of the World Center's envelope around the volume of the Twin Towers articulates its volume as a set of interstitial spaces that escape a singular spatial hierarchy and homogeneous relation between the built environment and its inhabitants.

The formal and spatial articulation of the scheme promotes a spatial politic of temporal individual and collective experiences. The tension between formal and organisational ambiguous articulation grants, in every location, a unique experience of a sensuous figure or surface in formation and extends thus the question of form to the question of experience. The scheme's surface geometry articulates spaces, while its material make-up and striated articulation – similar to that of the previous Twin Towers – enables a modulated transparency of both the skin and the spaces within and beyond it.

As the scheme proposes a 'thickening' of the space of existing buildings by adding layers around them, there arises a need for rethinking the question of daylight in deep structures. By questioning an equal need for daylight, differentiated interior habitats can be articulated instead. Rainforests and the oceans can serve as organisational models, where even in the lowest and darkest regions micro-ecologies flourish.

A secondary local form-finding process focused on the regulation of light conditions within an established range. Differentiated spatial material and ambient articulations are mobilised to yield emergent social, representational and habitational arrangements. This argument relates to Achim Menges's discussion of morpho-ecologies and indicates that form finding and form adaptation must be understood in relation to dynamic synergies between material form and behaviour, the habitats determined by those synergies, constituted by a differentiated condition-based environment and the contingent influence of inhabitants and emergent activities that need to be registered and fed back into the continual form-evolving process.

For the development of the World Center this implies that the design teams that will articulate the material form of the spatial pockets need to set out their own specific parameters for form finding and adaptation that then also need to be coordinated to the extent that spatial, structural, topological and experiential consistency is achieved, which will require some thinking and innovation in terms of form-finding criteria throughout the different phases of the project development, as well as shared knowledge and data bases. Consistency and alteration of form-finding parameters across design development phases and scales need to be carefully negotiated with the many design teams at work.

Finally, it is important to point out that a discussion of the evolution of form-finding design method and of its output would remain incomplete without a reflection on the consequences for architectural practice. To tackle complex and inclusive form-finding processes as a form of architectural practice implies the rethinking of some of its most deeply entrenched dogmas. This includes the redefinition of architectural services from the provision of singular and finite design solutions to the tactical management of time-based material processes across scales and milieus.

Quite obviously this discussion will yield a strong impact on the content of contracts and thus on the architect and client relationship. Instead of the common item-based contract, architectural services would have to be recognised as equally time-based as the continual design process. Client and architect would have to periodically update the performance requirements of a 'project' and feed this information back into the formative process that, as outlined as the third task of form finding, concerns itself with adaptation of material systems and processes in context. This discussion is particularly interesting given that architecture as a practice promotes innovation in approaches to design, but is very conservative in its resistance to the evolution of its concerns and modus operandi. Yet, need we worry, since nothing retains its form? *D*

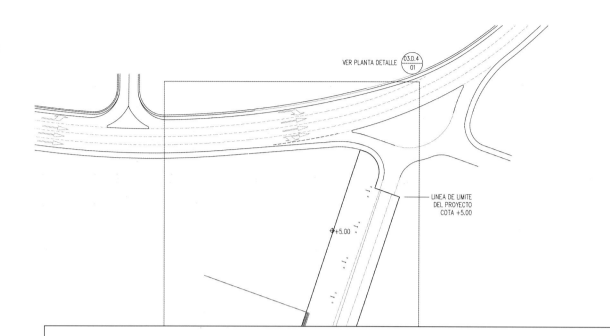

VER PLANTA DETALLE 03.D.4 / 01

LINEA DE LIMITE
DEL PROYECTO
COTA +5.00

⊕+5.00

Types, Style and

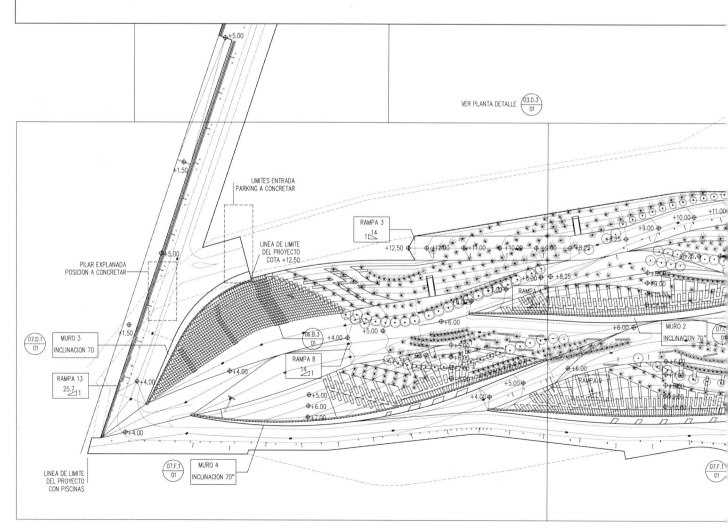

⊕+5.00

VER PLANTA DETALLE 03.D.3 / 01

+1.50

LIMITES ENTRADA
PARKING A CONCRETAR

RAMPA 3
1 14

+10.00   +11.00

+9.00

LINEA DE LIMITE
DEL PROYECTO
COTA +12.50

+12.50   ⊕ +12.00   +11.00   +10.00   +9.00   +8.25   8.25   +8.25

PILAR EXPLANADA
POSICION A CONCRETAR

⊕+5.00

+8.00   +8.25

RAMPA

+8.00
+9.00

07.D.1 / 01   MURO 3
INCLINACION 70

+1.50

06.B.3 / 01   +4.00

+5.00

+6.00

MURO 2
INCLINACION 70°   07.

RAMPA 13
25.7   11

⊕ +4.00

RAMPA 8
14   11

+6.00

+5.00

+6.00

RAMPA

+6.00

⊕+5.00

+5.00

+4.00

⊕+4.00

⊕+7.00

LINEA DE LIMITE
DEL PROYECTO
CON PISCINAS

07.F.1 / 01   MURO 4
INCLINACION 70°

07.F.1 / 01

Farshid Moussavi and Alejandro Zaera Polo of Foreign Office Architects, in conversation with the Emergence and Design Group, discuss the systematisation of their work by phylogenesis and species, and the implications that this new paradigm has for the methods and techniques that they have refined during their 10 years in practice.

Phylogenesis

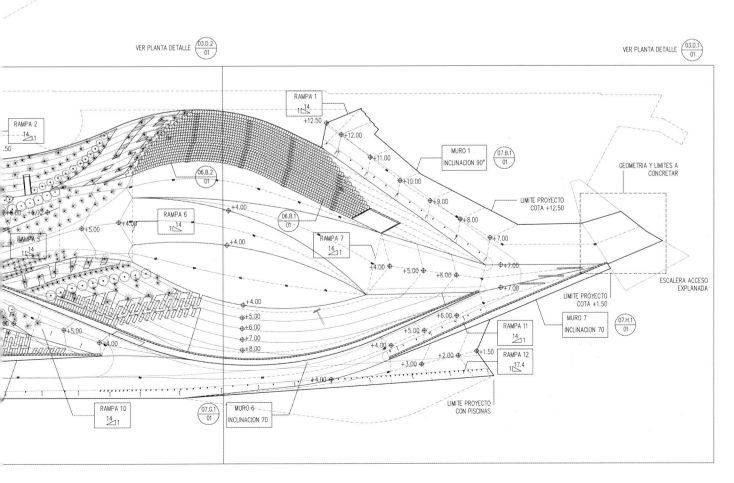

In recent exhibitions and publications, Foreign Office Architects (FOA) has systematised the representation of its work in the form of a phylogram, a means of reviewing the firm's body of work over the 10 years it has been in practice. A phylogram, or phylogenetic tree, is a device of classification in biology which is used for systematic studies of evolutionary history and the relationships among organisms that have common ancestors. In this case the phylogram operates to identify consistency across the different design processes, projects and the overall body of the architects' work.

'FOA grew very much out of the culture of "nonstyle", but we have lately realised that there were certain features that appeared in various projects. This helped us to accelerate processes and improve on discoveries that we had made,

and we began to understand style as the improvement of techniques and operations through repetition in different projects. Out of that we started to systematise these features.'

In a design studio at Columbia University taught by Farshid Moussavi and Alejandro Zaera Polo, entitled Back to the Hardcore, the pair renewed their interest in types as a pool of raw material to work from. Departing from this interest, they began to look at their projects as variations of a lineage, as a tree that includes all the different projects and which can be used to trace a history of ideas and of forms, of knowledge that can become operative when an opportunity appears.

'We had been experimenting in the Columbia studio and with the students we have in Vienna. We talk about the importance of language in architecture, and working across cultures or what we call "ecosystems", and what we extract from them. Typology provides raw material, a kind of "genetic pool" that we carry with us. We regard types not as fixed structures but as open organisational structures that we can proliferate and modify. The intention of using phyllotaxis to systematise the work was initially a postrationalisation, providing coherence and clarity for exhibitions and publications. We have used phyllotaxis three times. The first time was for the exhibition in Tokyo, the second one was for our show in Vienna and the third one was for the show at the ICA in London. We are not developing the tree in an instrumental way at the moment. It represents for us an initial idea of a taxonomic approach to understanding and systematising our work.'

If the phylogram is to be an instrument, the question is how it can grow. Each new project can establish a new distinct and separate lineage on a branching tree. On the other hand, crossover between projects can produce a new project as a direct offspring of the form or from the methodology of previous generations. FOA has initially used the phylogram to become conscious of relationships and repetitions within the firm's work, but the architects also consider that it might be developed into an operational tool for the 'breeding' of new projects. In this sense the phylogram can be used to organise formal operations and rule-based processes for 'breeding' between projects rather than a more literal hybridisation of forms.

'Our phylogenetic paradigm has not yet become operative. It is latent in our operating mode, and we are somehow trying to surface it, but it is very difficult to turn it into a methodology. At the moment the tree is more of a representation than an operative device. It has not yet generated a methodology and so we have not been able to make it operative. One immediate use of the phylogram is that it allows us to assess the progress of our work. This is important in the light of iteration-based methodology and research. The problem is that the development of methodology takes so much time that, finally, the project

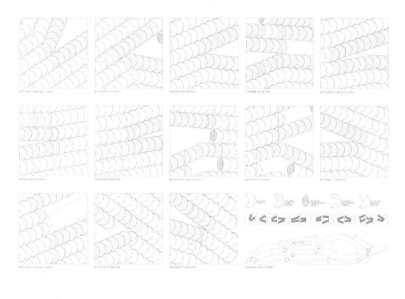

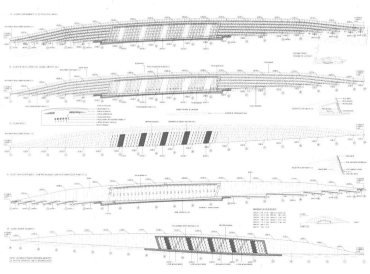

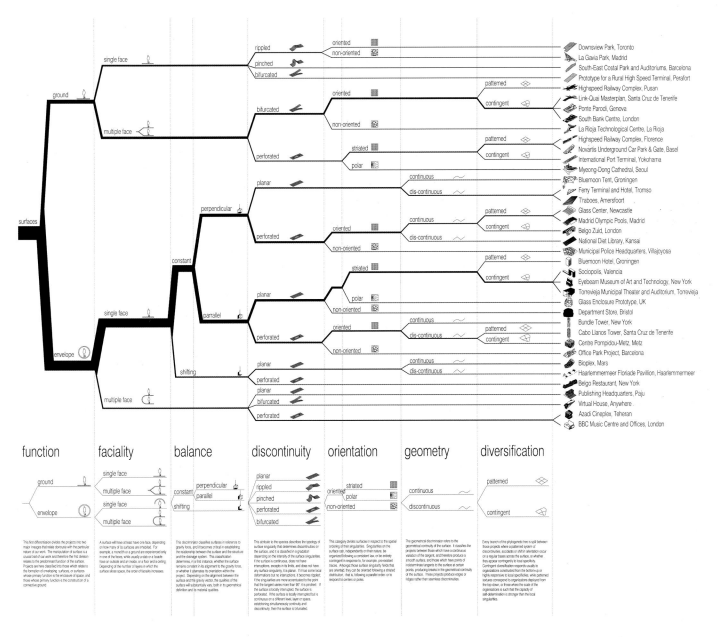

The phylogenetic tree diagram includes the following project listings (right side):

- Downsview Park, Toronto
- La Gavia Park, Madrid
- South-East Costal Park and Auditoriums, Barcelona
- Prototype for a Rural High Speed Terminal, Perafort
- Highspeed Railway Complex, Pusan
- Link-Quai Masterplan, Santa Cruz de Tenerife
- Ponte Parodi, Genova
- South Bank Centre, London
- La Rioja Technological Centre, La Rioja
- Highspeed Railway Complex, Florence
- Novartis Underground Car Park & Gate, Basel
- International Port Terminal, Yokohama
- Myeong-Dong Cathedral, Seoul
- Bluemoon Tent, Groningen
- Ferry Terminal and Hotel, Tromso
- Traboes, Amersfoort
- Glass Center, Newcastle
- Madrid Olympic Pools, Madrid
- Belgo Zuid, London
- National Diet Library, Kansai
- Municipal Police Headquarters, Villajoyosa
- Bluemoon Hotel, Groningen
- Sociopolis, Valencia
- Eyebeam Museum of Art and Technology, New York
- Torrevieja Municipal Theater and Auditorium, Torrevieja
- Glass Enclosure Prototype, UK
- Department Store, Bristol
- Bundle Tower, New York
- Cabo Llanos Tower, Santa Cruz de Tenerife
- Centre Pompidou-Metz, Metz
- Office Park Project, Barcelona
- Bioplex, Mars
- Haarlemmermeer Floriade Pavillion, Haarlemmermeer
- Belgo Restaurant, New York
- Publishing Headquarters, Paju
- Virtual House, Anywhere
- Azadi Cineplex, Teheran
- BBC Music Centre and Offices, London

function

ground
envelope

This first differentiation divides the projects into two major lineages that relate obviously with the particular nature of our work. The manipulation of surface is a crucial trait of our work and therefore the first division relates to the predominant function of the surface. Projects are here classified into those which relate to the formation of enveloping, surfaces, or surfaces whose primary function is the enclosure of space, and those whose primary function is the construction of a connective ground.

faciality

single face
multiple face
single face
multiple face

A surface will have at least have one face, depending on how many of its surfaces are inhabited. For example, a monolith or a ground are experienced only in one of the faces, while usually a slab or a facade have an outside and an inside, or a floor and a ceiling. Depending on the number of layers in which the surface slices space, the order of faciality increases.

balance

perpendicular
constant
parallel
shifting

This discriminator classifies surfaces in reference to gravity force, and it becomes critical in establishing the relationship between the surface and the structure and the drainage system. This classification determines, in a first instance, whether the surface remains constant in its alignment to the gravity force, or whether it alternates its orientation within the project. Depending on the alignment between the surface and the gravity vector, the qualities of the surface will substantially vary, both in its geometrical definition and its material qualities.

discontinuity

planar
rippled
pinched
perforated
bifurcated

This attribute to the species describes the typology of surface singularity that determines discontinuities on the surface, and it is classified in a gradation depending on the intensity of the surface singularities. If the surface is continuous, does not have interruptions, excepts in its limits, and does not have any surface singularity, it is planar. If it has some local deformations but no interruptions, it becomes rippled; if the singularities are more accentuated to the point that the tangent varies more than 90°, it is pinched. If the surface is locally interrupted, the surface is perforated. If the surface is locally interrupted but is continuous on a different level, layer or space, establishing simultaneously continuity and discontinuity, then the surface is bifurcated.

orientation

oriented   striated / polar
non-oriented

This category divides surfaces in respect to the spatial ordering of their singularities. Singularities on the surface can, independently on their nature, be organized following a consistent law, or be entirely contingent in response to, for example, pre-existent traces. Amongst those surface singularity fields that are oriented, they can be oriented following a striated distribution, that is, following a parallel order- or to respond to centers or poles.

geometry

continuous
discontinuous

The geometrical discriminator refers to the geometrical continuity of the surface. It classifies the projects between those which have a continuous variation of the tangent, and therefore produce a smooth surface, and those which have points of indeterminate tangents to the surface at certain points, producing breaks in the geometrical continuity of the surface. Those projects produce edges or ridges rather than seamless discontinuities.

diversification

patterned
contingent

Every branch of the phylogenetic tree is split between those projects where a patterned system of discontinuities, accidents or shift in orientation occur on a regular bases across the surface, or whether they appear contingently to local specificity. Contingent diversification responds usually to organizations constructed from the bottom-up or highly responsive to local specificities, while patterned textures correspond to organizations deployed from the top-down, or those where the scale of the organisations is such that the capacity of self-determination is stronger than the local singularities.

Top right
FOA's phylogenetic tree. Projects are initially differentiated into two categories: surfaces whose primary function is to enclose space and surfaces whose primary function is the construction of a connective ground.

Middle right
The bundle tower is a new high-rise protoype described as a species in its most diagrammatic form, grown in a generic ecosystem, and awaiting the specificity of a situation.

Bottom right
Structural type according to number of floors.

becomes legitimised only by the fact that it is consistent with the methodology. And at the end you still need to resort to typologies and history of architecture that are independent from the product of these processes.

'If every new project uses a mutation of a previous project, there is no process of discovery. What do you begin with as raw material: nothing or a certain thing? So, if we decide to mutate this or that, the decision is made before the environment introduces a completely new lineage into the tree. It is important to develop mechanisms of verification, no matter how much data you have and how much complexity we bring into the project. We directly pick up what is there and work with it. In the design for Yokohama we prioritised passenger flows, whereas for the Southeast Coastal Park in Barcelona the distribution of programme was informed by an analysis of the required sport and leisure activities that allowed the topography of the landscape to be generated.

'For the World Trade Center we looked at the evolution of high-rise buildings, emerging from

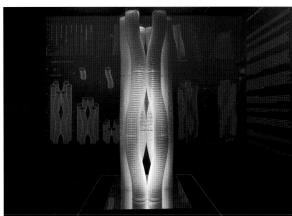

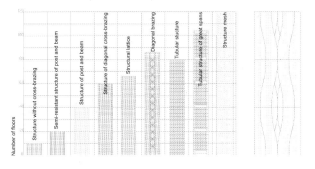

37

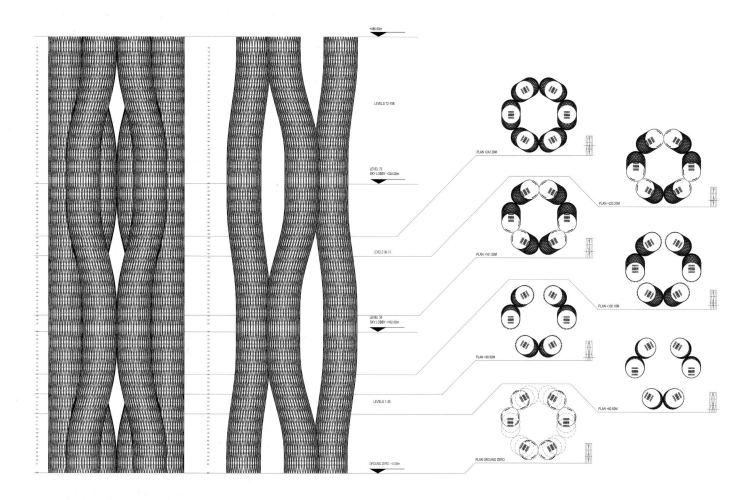

the pages of *Neufert*, and the Petronas and Sears towers. This is a very important project for us because it is the first to emerge from a reflection on typology. It was about understanding the history of the type and producing something directly out of that history. In all of the projects the aim was to look for generative potentials. In order to discover new aesthetics and new forms, we set up a process from which we look for emergent possibilities. If we have to make an auditorium, why blind ourselves to all the previous experiments with auditoriums? We should look at auditoriums, disassemble them and look at them as rules of projection and angles of seating, as raw materials that we can grow in particular ways.'

FOA formulates particular questions at the beginning of a project, and uses them to initiate the process of generation. It is a shaping of precisely framed interests, quite different to setting out open-ended research that may or may not end with a project. Projects always involve working with others, and it is apparent that FOA has a wide set of interests and some expertise in other disciplines. The question arises how

collaboration with experts will affect the production of the 'raw material' for design.

'Collaborations are only interesting when they become generative. We are interested in all of the systems that can be incorporated into a project. You need to understand a certain minimum about these systems and processes to know that they have material implications. Environmental engineering is one that seems to repeat. In the Toronto Park project we developed a new ecosystem, redirecting water by manipulating the space of the site.'

It is interesting to note that Frei Otto in his conversation with the Emergence and Design Group, earlier in this issue, claimed that there are certain systems and behaviours that can only be investigated and proved through physical modelling, particularly tensile structures and minimal surfaces for which mathematical models are not comprehensively developed. He argued that it is only possible to develop and test such structures and their behaviour in physical models. FOA holds quite different views and the roles of physical models and data models in the firm's work are distinct.

'We don't do physical models to generate projects as we prefer to work with digital models in the design process. The form is developed gradually,

Above
Horizontal section elevation.

Opposite, top
Vertical section detail.

Opposite, bottom
Sky-lobby transfer diagram.

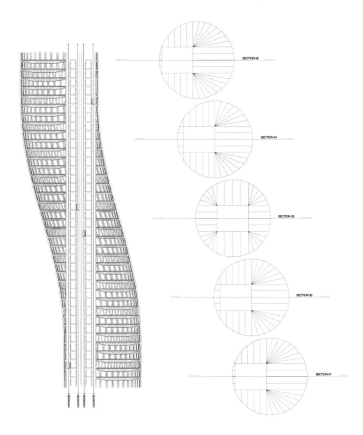

SECTION

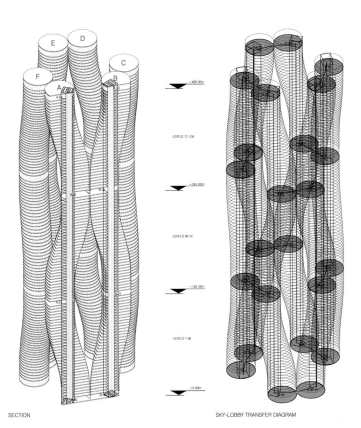

SECTION   SKY-LOBBY TRANSFER DIAGRAM

incrementally involving and incorporating various pieces of information over time, throughout the generation of the project. Everything we need to do we can do on the computer. We are familiar with the interface with the computer so we trust it. Physical models come at the end of the design process, as presentation models for the client or for a show. Physical models would only be interesting to us if they would help us to understand the geometric logic that underlies them. We have not found ways of working with physical models that are as efficient as working with digital models. If we had more staff we might work much more with physical models, if it were possible for the physical model development to keep pace with the development of the digital models. The more tools you can work with the more possibilities you have. The problem with insisting on the use of physical models is that they exclude working with nonvisual parameters, for example circulation or environmental issues. The computer can model visual and nonvisual information.'

The working techniques of FOA over many years indicate a strong interest in methods based on incremental development. It seems logical to suggest that a more explicit use of evolutionary computational techniques could be part of the architects' future research for the practice.

'As to our plans for research, if we had unlimited resources we would set up a research group in the office that does not have the pressure of delivering projects, perhaps investigating the possibility of using the phylogenetic tree as a generative tool. Evolutionary generation is an incredibly promising field, and if we had the resources we would also research this approach. In the Yokohama project there was a moment in which we had to develop a piece of software that would evolve form, because there was a problem of optimisation of symmetry of pieces. Similarly, the design for the Southeast Coastal Park in Barcelona required this kind of computational approach to achieve a suitable relation between plantation, irrigation and drainage. These were, in a way, evolutionary design approaches, because we set up a system of rules that were competing.

But this is something we can do only in certain parts of a project. We don't think that one can solve all architectural problems by using these generative systems. It would be completely mad; neither pragmatic nor efficient. You have to rely on your experience as an architect, on your acquired knowledge to focus the experiment, and then in some areas of the project these methods will be viable. We think that to generate each project from scratch is against the logic of efficiency of production. It will turn the project into a nightmare, with every little piece of the project being infinite in its possibilities. The closer you get the more it opens up.' ∆

Fit Fabric:
Versatility Through Redundancy and Differentiation

There is a need to rethink the design of high-rise buildings, to find an approach that integrates structure and behaviour into material systems that are adapted to vertical urbanism. Michael Weinstock, Achim Menges and Michael Hensel, founding partners of the **Emergence and Design Group**, argue the case for considering high-rise buildings as surface structures. They discuss the need for flexure and stiffness in the context of natural structures that provide models for geometry, pattern, form and behaviour. Their evolutionary process has produced a design for high-rise structures in which a helical structural system and an intelligent skin are integrated into a versatile material system.

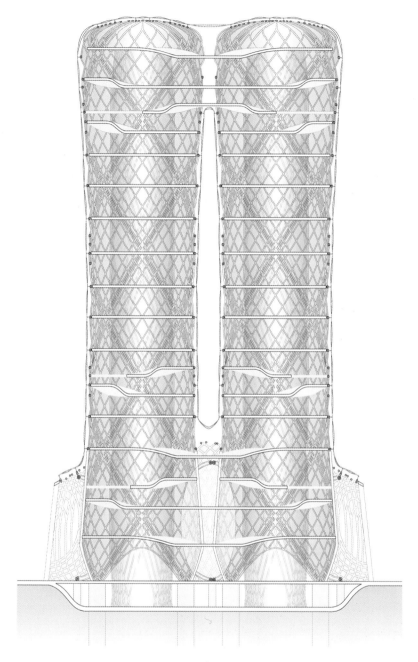

'Will we not attain a more satisfactory insight into the mysterious architecture of the formative process by looking into the following question: How does a surrounding element, with its various specific characteristics, affect the general form we have been studying? How does the form, both determined and determinant, assert itself against these elements? What manner of hard parts, soft parts, interior parts, and exterior parts are created in the form by this effect? And what is wrought by the elements through all their diversity of height and depth, region and climate?
— Johann Wolfgang von Goethe,
Writings on Morphology, 1817

Fitness Through Flexure

Two notions dominate the traditional approach of engineering to the design of structure: stiffness and efficiency. Stiffness implies that structural members are optimised so that they do not easily bend, and members are arranged into whole structures that are rigid and inflexible. Efficiency characterises the preferred mode of achieving structural stiffness with a minimum amount of material and energy. In this approach, any elasticity of the material from which it is made must be minimised, and elastic deformation of the structure under load is carefully calculated.

The structure of tall buildings exemplifies this approach to engineering, so that the central core supports much of the weight of the structure and its imposed load. Floor plates and beams connect the central core to surrounding exterior columns, each conducting a small part of the load to the ground and preventing the building from overturning or sliding when exposed to strong lateral forces such as wind or earthquakes. The horizontal structure of the floors braces the entire building by tying inner core and outer frame together.

Analysis of the collapse of the World Trade Center towers reveals that while the steel-mesh exterior frame was highly robust, the steel trusses that supported the floors may have been more fragile, and that the central core was not designed to handle very strong lateral forces. Another governmental study concluded that the primary cause for structural failure was the intense heat of the fire that broke out, which softened and deformed the floor trusses. And a further study pointed out that all these conclusions did not take into account the effects of torque, and that the buildings could have toppled at the moment of impact if their frames had not flexed to absorb much of the energy of the impact. It seems likely that the combination of severe local tearing and material deformation under heat produced a sequence that was catastrophic.

It follows that the calculation of elastic behaviour in a whole structure is more difficult to model than has been previously assumed, and catastrophic events combine several forces that interact to produce a nonlinear acceleration of effects. Also, the ability to tolerate flexure may be more beneficial for structures than had been previously assumed. The combination of the need for flexure and sufficient stiffness for stability requires the criteria of efficiency to be rethought. Models of surface structures that exhibit the ability to flex without collapse exist in human and natural artefacts. Baskets, for example, can accept several local disruptions without collapsing globally. Baskets have a high degree of redundancy, having more material than is strictly necessary for simple loads, and rely on friction in place of joints. All living structures have a very high degree of redundancy, which is what enables them to be adaptive. Joints are notably different from traditionally engineered joints, provided only for articulation and even then material is continuous right through the joint.

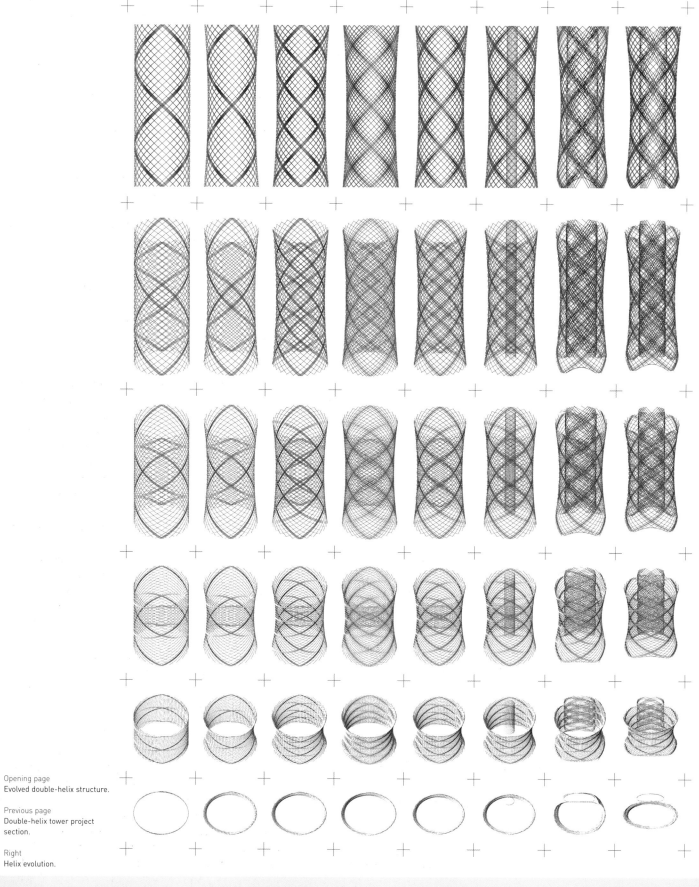

Opening page
Evolved double-helix structure.

Previous page
Double-helix tower project
section.

Right
Helix evolution.

Adopting these strategies of design for tall buildings will make a radical change to their performance. The total amount of material involved will not be excessively increased, for whilst there will be many more members, each individual member will be very much smaller in section.

Cylindrical Morphologies and Helices

There are natural structures that have a cylindrical morphology, that display a robust and flexible structural performance that is provided mainly within the skin without any internal ribs or columns. These structures achieve a wide range of performances and functions through the organisation of their components – fibres and matrix materials – in 3-D assemblies, despite the fact that fibres have low compressive strength and are prone to buckling. Cylinders are generally particularly prone to buckling. Natural evolution has provided several successful strategies for surface structures, including shape-optimised morphologies, and the arrangement of components in complex hierarchies to provide multiple load-path vectors. The Emergence and Design Group is exploring the development of architectural-scale surface structures that achieve their coherence by the organisation of very simple components into differentiated bundles and braids.

Geometry is essential in natural and computational morphogenesis. It provides the set of boundary constraints that inform the global configuration of a developed form as well as the local rules and organising principles for self-organisation during morphogenesis. The initial research into generic patterns in natural systems suggested that the helix be selected for this evolutionary experiment.

Spiral helices occur in dynamic configurations at all scales in the physical world. They appear in enormous energy systems such as spiral galaxies that have central regions thousands of light years across. Helices are immediately visible in geophysical systems such as the atmosphere or oceans, in the dynamic vortices of hurricanes, tornadoes, storms and whirlpools. In living forms spiral helices are found in, for example, the arrangement of protein molecules in DNA and the geometry of pine cones, sunflowers and the florets of broccoli. Xylem vessels in plants are the slender tubes that transport water and solutes up from the roots into the stem and leaves. Spiral bands of lignin reinforce xylems, and the spiral geometry allows the tubes to elongate and grow. In many plants the arrangement of the leaves around the stem corresponds with the Fibonacci number sequence, which appears to maximise the space available for each leaf to receive the optimal degree of sunlight.

Development of the Genotype

The evolutionary process of the Emergence and Design Group's research project began with the 'seed', or primary input, of the simplest industrial component – the section of a steel tube 150 millimetres in diameter. This was swept along a helix to the bounding limits of the mathematical 'environment', which was defined by the planning constraints and dimensions of a competition site for a tall building. The single, helical tubular member was 'bundled' by generating copies rotated around the originating centre. This established a 60-metre double helix of 10 tubular members deployed in two bundles, which was further evolved by generating a counter-rotated inner layer. In the next generation four bundles were selected, each with its outer and inner group in counter rotations. In successive generations inner and outer layers of members were deployed in the quadrants between the bundles. The structure at this stage of evolution has 80 members arranged in two concentric contiguous layers. Forces were applied to the global geometry, producing a population of variant forms, and from these a single form with the base and top flared, and the waist slightly narrowed, was selected.

The development of the genotype continued by relaxing the geometrical rule of parallel construction planes for the inner and outer layer of helices. This resulted in more complex geometrical relations between the planes of the outer helices and inner helices, which evolved in curved planes with nonuniform distances between them. The curved planes of the helices became strongly differentiated,

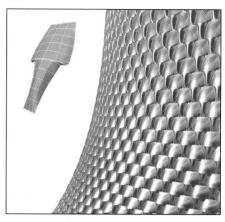

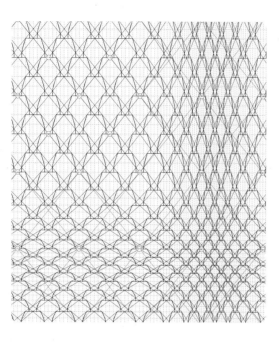

Right
Skin-panel geometry:
algorithmic differentiation.

Far right
Skin-panel adaptability.

Below
Skin panel.

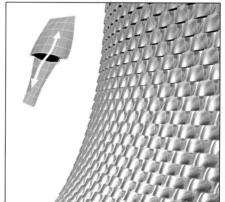

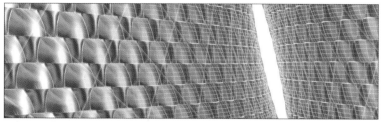

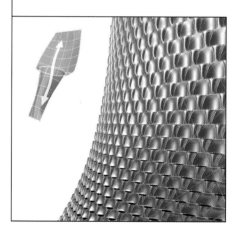

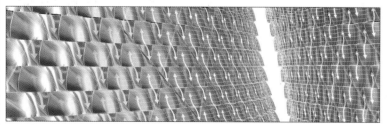

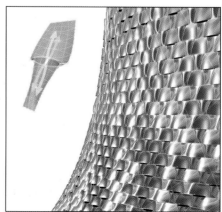

sometimes quite far apart, sometimes touching and occasionally penetrating each other. A reciprocal development within the planes changed the initial arrangement of equal distances between individual helical members, so that varied distances between individuals appeared, and finally intersections between individuals. A higher level of structural organisation emerged, in which microstructures intersect, wrap around each other, bundle and unbundle. The complexity suggests a new spatial organisation and structural capacities may be enabled by the phenotype. Floor plates, for example, may be more three-dimensionally articulated and less symmetrical than in conventional tower structures, and may even be volumetric.

Development of the Phenotype

The development of the phenotype is driven by exposure of the geometry to environmental forces, a process that encourages twins, multiples, and aggregations of forms that increase structural capacity by sharing and distribution of loads – not speciation but variation within one population of geometries.

The building envelope was developed from a digital study and finite element analysis of the tessellated surface geometry of a custard apple. The skin of the fruit must maintain its structural integrity, resisting the pressure of the swelling material inside. The panels all have the same form but size is varied, and tessellation results in a surprisingly low number of variations required for the complex double curvatures.

The building envelope is considered as an integral system of structure and environmental regulator-panels that are adaptive in geometry and performance. The differentiation of the geometry of the panels follows a similar logic to the differentiation of the helices – all have the same form and geometric logic but the size is varied through a limited number of parametric changes. These few parametric changes allow the form of the panel to adapt to the changing curvature and varying density of the helical structure through a simple algorithm. The organisation of the structural interface, the connection between the helices and panel regions, is local. This maintains coherence between the different geometric hierarchies and has the capacity to adjust to global changes in geometry.

The skin is activated by a micropneumatic structure. It achieves its kinetic capacities through differential pressure in a capillary

system of pneumatic actuator cells that are distributed between the inner, centre and outer membranes. Differential pressure in capillary layers triggers the change from convex to concave geometry by the differential expansion and contraction of layers. Synchronised changes from convex to concave geometry in a panel allow the regulation of light reflection between the inner and outer membrane, and the insulating volume of the enclosed air space.

Alternating the changes to the geometry of the lower and upper half of a panel regulates the fresh air ventilation and directs light transmission. Differential pressure between pneumatic chambers allows for movement of the interfacing membrane. Patterns of photovoltaic cells printed on the membranes collect a secondary solar energy gain, which can be collected from the entire surface and used to feed the microcompressor that produces the air pressure of the pneumatic actuator cells in each half panel. All the energy necessary to maintain the air pressure and to operate the regulator valves of the pneumatic panels is sourced, stored and managed locally by very simple microprocessors, microcompressors and high-capacity accumulators. There is no need to draw on a central energy supply, which increases the reliability and efficiency of the system and lowers production and maintenance costs.

Environmental data, from interior and exterior, is collected by local sensors and processed locally. The activity of individual panels is entirely local and is a response to local stimuli. Direct operation by users is local, affecting an individual panel or a surface region of the building. The self-learning capacity of the simple panel processing units also happens locally. Each panel is independently responsive, capable of modulating the passage of light, heat and air through it in both directions, and managing its own energy economy. No remote central processing is used for instruction: sensing and activation are embedded functions in each individual panel, and multiple links between them provide the means for a distributed intelligence from which a complex global performance emerges. The exterior appearance will be constantly changing, with small variations in angles and transparencies producing an animated and subtle surface.

The integration of the structure and the responsive envelope offer an extended performative capacity. Increasing levels of differentiation of the helices yields the potential for changes to the spatial organisation by the ability to accept relatively free distribution of floors. The responsive building envelope makes it possible to differentiate interior microclimates, both in response to the diverse needs of the inhabitants and to the overall energy balance of

Membrane Skins

The tessellated surface of a custard apple fruit
helps to maintain its structural integrity against
the pressure of the swelling flesh as it ripens
inside. A morphological analysis by Birger
Sevaldson, of the Oslo School of Architecture,
was carried out with a Minolta Vivid 900 scanner
that registers not only the overall form but also
its texture and the RGB value of its colouration.
The images here show (from top to bottom) the
different stages of the scanning process and the
subsequent fitting together of the various scans
into a coherent digital model. During the process
of scanning the ripe fruit began to break open,
a natural process that exposes and distributes
the 50 to 70 seeds. Analysis of the skin and
volume during the irreversible movement was
done by four scans taken sequentially. From
these four scans, digital 3-D models were
extracted and rapid prototype models (selective
laser sintering) models were made of each scan,
providing physical models for study. The cracks
that occurred in the membrane tissue as it
dried out did not follow the edges of the surface
tessellation. During its growth the pressure
of the fluid in the soft pulp of the interior
pressurises the membrane skin of the fruit.
As the fruit dries, the pressure equilibrium
between interior and surface is lost and the
pre-stress in the membrane becomes
increasingly excessive. Water loss in the
membrane causes the fibres to shrink, which
increases the tension beyond the capacity
of the material to maintain its integrity.
The process took several hours, but the same
process can produce explosive movements in
other fruits.

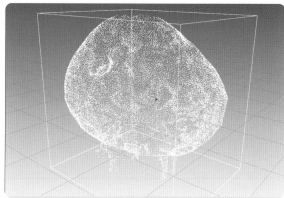

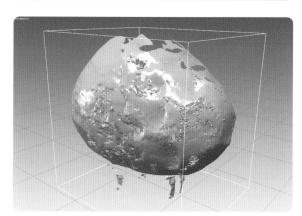

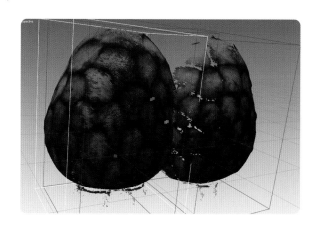

Spiral Phyllotaxis

In spiral phyllotaxis there are two main
families of spiral helices called parastichies.
These may either be organised symmetrically
or asymmetrically with respect to the number
of counter-rotating spirals. The arrangement
of the scales of pine cones is asymmetric.
Two arrangements of ascending spirals grow
outward from the point of attachment to the
branch: eight spirals ascend the cone in a
clockwise direction, while 13 spirals ascend
more steeply in a counterclockwise direction.
The number of spirals or helices in the two
families tends to be two consecutive elements
in the Fibonacci sequence. These special types
are referred to as Fibonacci phyllotaxis, which
yields optimised packing arrangements of the
respective units. However, the magnolia cone
is arranged in a more symmetrical manner.
The same number of spirals ascends in the
clockwise and counterclockwise directions.
The scales all have the same form but size
varies according to location on the spiral,
and tessellation results in a surprisingly low
number of variations required for the complex
double-curved surfaces. A magnolia cone
was 3-D-scanned with the help of Professor
Birger Sevaldson. From the 3-D scan, a
digital model was derived and analysed
by Neri Oxman, with respect to the helical
organisation of the exterior surface of the
cone. ⌀

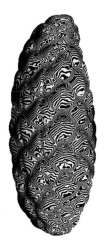

Evolutionary Computation and Artificial Life in Architecture: Exploring the Potential of Generative and Genetic Algorithms as Operative Design Tools

The current groundwork in evolutionary computation and generative computation presents promising potentials for applications in architecture. In this article, Dr Una-May O'Reilly, Martin Hemberg and Achim Menges examine the capacity of software developments that operate at the intersection of architecture, artificial intelligence, artificial life, engineering and material science. Two morphogenetic design experiments explore the application of combined generative and genetic algorithms as operative design tools.

Nature's complex forms and systems arise from evolutionary processes. In addition, living forms grow, and growth is a complex process, intertwining contributions of the genotype with the variable contributions of environment and phenotypic dependencies. In nature the genotype comprises the genetic constitution of an individual, while the phenotype is the product of the interactions between the genotype and the environment. The emergent properties and capacities of natural forms stem from the generative processes that work upon successive versions of the genome. This genome is compact data that is transformed into biomass of increasing structural complexity.

A compelling goal is to instrumentalise the natural processes of evolution and growth, to model essential features of emergence and then to combine these within a computational framework. The aim is to apply this instrument as a generative design tool that can produce complex and adaptive architectural forms. The current computational groundwork in evolutionary computation and generative computation present promising potentials to reach this goal. Evolutionary algorithms, traditionally utilised for optimisation, are now also instantiated for their adaptive qualities. They permit performative morphological

processes, adaptiogenesis[1] and inherent novelty to be investigated in bounds greatly superseding hand-driven experimentation. Furthermore, evolutionary computation not only allows many different instantiations by automating the repetitive, but yields novel representations and process descriptions of instrumental performance-driven evolutionary processes that derive complex emergent structure.

In the following paragraphs both the potential and the current limits of evolutionary computation in architecture will be discussed, in the context of the underlying operative structure, organisation and application of an advanced software system. Una-May O'Reilly and Martin Hemberg were part of a research group at MIT that included computer scientists and architects. They examined the potential synergy between architecture, artificial intelligence, artificial life, engineering and material science, and developed prototype software design tools embedded within an existing CAD system.

Integrating evolutionary computation, generative computation and physical environment modelling techniques, Genr8 is the latest instantiation of such a design tool. It uses a population-based adaptation akin to evolution and a generative algorithm akin to growth. Genr8 is a unique combination of grammatical evolution (the evolutionary computation algorithm) and extended Map Lindenmayer systems[2] (the generative algorithm). Implemented as a plug-in for Alias Wavefront's 3-D

Opposite
Multiplanar surface articulation: through the mutual adaptiogenesis of geometric fitness criteria and geometric articulation the morphogenetic process yields an ever-increasing complexity of two co-evolved surfaces that nevertheless remains coherent with the logics of the material system and manufacturing with a laser cutter.

EXPERIMENT 1

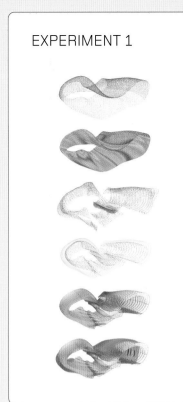

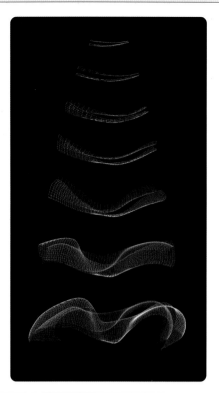

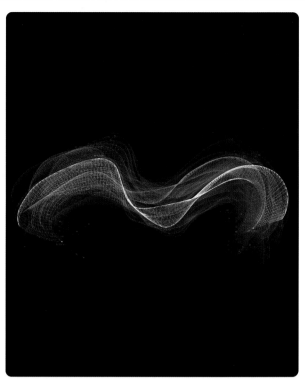

modeller Maya, and based on confluent dynamics of selection, variation and inheritance, Genr8 enables a simulation of stochastic, evolutionary and environment-based structures and surface geometries.

In order to realise the generative power of this evolutionary computing tool it is essential to understand its theoretical framework and its computational environment.

Genr8 allows the exploration and development of surface geometries in 3-D space that have virtual environmental conditions. The exploration is enabled by an evolutionary module that produces populations of surfaces in many generations, and the development is governed by an algorithm that mimics organic growth. Initially, every surface is an equilateral polygon. Subsequently, each surface grows larger and more complex as it is repeatedly revised according to a unique set of rules. The growth process is inspired by Lindenmayer systems (L-systems), which achieve form by exploiting the interaction of two components: the definition, a seed of the form and rewriting rules that specify how elements of the form change, and a graphical process that repeatedly reinterprets the rules with respect to the current form.

The specific growth model implemented in Genr8 is provided by Hemberg-Extended-Map-Lindenmayer-System (HEMLS), which extends Map L-systems by allowing for the growth of surfaces in 3-D space. It also includes more complex grammars and a simulated physical environment. Consequently, HEMLS generates surfaces that are grown inclusively rather than

incrementally, since all parts of the surface are modified during the entire process. The surface is constructed through a bottom-up process in which all parts respond to local interactions and the environment. The surface is represented by a graph data structure that consists of a set of edges, vertices and regions. Since all edges can be rewritten throughout the entire growth process, all parts of the surface change continuously. These interactions are complex and the interpretation of the HEMLS is nonlinear, so the outcome of the growth process is open-ended and unpredictable. Phenotypic outcomes are thus influenced by both genotypic specifications and environmental conditions. When combining a growth process with form generation, it is imperative to situate the system within the context of a virtual environment – in the case of Genr8, one that has gravity, boundaries and attractors. Using Genr8, a designer can specify the environment prior to using the tool, and this has a significant impact on the growth process.

The combination of generative algorithm with an evolutionary algorithm makes Genr8 an interesting design tool. Computer scientists have been interested in evolution for decades, and created algorithmic paradigms[3] driven by selection, inheritance and variation, and other operators. Evolutionary computation has, to date, been mainly applied in optimisation domains. However, it also encodes a discovery-oriented and adaptive process that is well suited for a design tool. In Genr8 a population of individual designs can be generated and tested to find the fittest of these, which are then recombined and modified to produce improved 'descendent' designs that integrate preferred 'ancestral' features in a nonlinear fashion.[4] In Genr8, some evaluation criteria are explicitly quantifiable and capture local and global

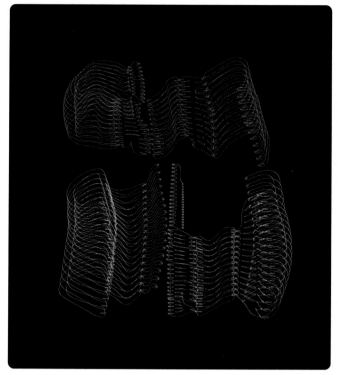

Above left
Coplanar arrangement of
multiplanar sections.

Above middle
Digital model evolved by a
digital morphogenetic process
using Genr8.

Above right
Intricate geometric relations
between multiplanar sectional
components and co-evolved
overall surfaces.

Notes
1 Adaptiogenesis is the process
of continuously producing new
adaptations. Adaptation is
defined as the process of
adjustment of an individual to
environmental conditions based
on evolutionary modifications.
2 Przemyslaw Prusinkiewicz
and Aristid Lindenmayer, *The
Algorithmic Beauty of Plants*,
Springer-Verlag (New York), 1990.
3 Essential sources for the
development of evolutionary
computation include the following:
L Fogel, A J Owens and M J
Walsh, *Artificial Intelligence
Through Simulated Evolution*,
John Wiley & Sons (New York),
1966; David E Goldberg, *Genetic
Algorithms in Search,
Optimization and Machine
Learning*, Addison-Wesley
(Reading, MA), 1989; John Koza,
*Genetic Programming: On the
Programming of Computers by
Means of Natural Selection*, MIT
Press (Cambridge, MA), 1992; Ingo
Rechenberg, *Evolution Strategy:
Optimization of Technical Systems
by Means of Biological Evolution*,
Fromman-Holzboog (Stuttgart),
1973; C Ryan, JJ Collins and M
O'Neill, *Lecture Notes in
Computer Science 1391*, First
European Workshop on Genetic
Programming, 1998.

features pertinent to surface geometry such as
size, smoothness, symmetry and subdivisions.

With the traditional approach to interactive
evolutionary computation (IEC) the user regulates
the fitness function by assigning fitness values
to each member of the population. By contrast,
Genr8 has an inbuilt automated fitness ranking.
This opens up the possibility for another, more
powerful interaction between the designer and
the evolutionary process through the
implementation of an interruption, intervention
and resumption (IIR) function. The IIR creates a
feedback between the internal evaluation of
Genr8 and other external performance criteria
within one evolutionary process. Interruption
allows the designer to stop the evolutionary
search at any time. At this point the designer
is free to export and analyse individuals, or
even entire populations, and intervene by
manipulating all settings and run-time
parameters, including the environment. Finally,
the user can resume the evolutionary search
where it was interrupted. This ability to change
parameters and map emergent phenotypic
characteristics back onto the genotype allows a
real performance-driven surface evolution that
is open to a wide range of external processes.

Genr8 has three key innovations. First, the
representations the software uses for the
surface as both a genome (a HEMLS) and a
phenotype (the surface); second, the process
within the evolutionary computation where the
genome is interpreted[5] repeatedly to generate a
surface; and third, the possibility of interrupting,
intervening, informing and resuming the
evolutionary process. It can therefore indicate

a potential use of evolutionary computation in
architecture that goes far beyond a simplistic
understanding of computers breeding geometries
overnight to be picked and selected by the designer
in the morning. Instead, the possibilities embedded
in the computational structure of Genr8 point towards
an integrated process of evolutionary adaptation,
continuous evaluation of individuals and a
systematisation of species. It suggests the recognition
and instrumentalisation of performative patterns of
complex surface geometries. Although additional
evaluation tools, for example advanced structural or
geometric analysis, have not been embedded in the
software system, the provision of IIR in Genr8 promotes
an inclusive evolutionary process that is capable of
allowing external analysis and evaluation to be fed
back into the form-generation process.

Two morphogenetic design experiments that make
extensive use of the generative and genetic engine of
Genr8 demonstrate the ability to combine evolutionary
computation with advanced digital evaluation and
modelling techniques, and the constraints of related
manufacturing processes.

The first experiment investigates the potential
combination of digitally evolved geometry and
computer-aided manufacturing with the aim of
achieving a coherency between manufacturing logic,
material constraints and increasingly complex
geometries. Evolutionary computation is used to
initiate a process that evolves two interlocking surfaces
through geometric fitness criteria. The experiment was
based on the understanding that the geometrical data
of surfaces with varying curvature can be described by
a system of tangential and perpendicular construction
planes, which is also suitable for subsequent
computer-aided laser cutting of sheet material.

EXPERIMENT 2

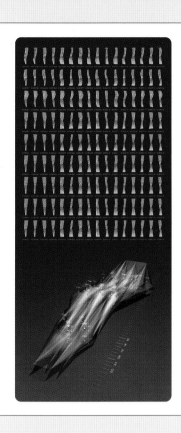

EXPERIMENT 1 + 2
Project credits

Software Development:
Dr. Una-May O'Reilly, Martin Hemberg,
Emergent Design Group, MIT

Morphogenetic Design Experiment 01
Achim Menges

Morphogenetic Design Experiment 02
AA Strawberry Bar: Achim Menges

The main aim of this research project was to extend the evolutionary dynamics of reproduction, mutation, competition and selection as design strategies. The potentials and limits from initial form generation to the actual manufacturing process were explored by shifting the investigation towards performative patterns that evolve as species across populations and successive generations whilst maintaining structural capacity and geometric characteristics.

4 In other words, among a population of surfaces, the fitter are more likely to be chosen as parents of the next generation. They pass on their genetic material, which is subject to variation. This variation is the blind mutation and crossover of the genomes.
5 The HEMLS is a Backus-Naur form (BNF) that is graphically interpreted within a 3-D environment with gravity, boundaries and attractors. Backus-Naur form is a metalanguage used for defining the syntax of formal languages, both for the developer of the language and for the user.
6 The surface normal is defined as a unit vector perpendicular to a local surface. It constitutes the first derivative of position by indicating how the measured surface location varies while indexing across a range map.

A number of geometric constraints were established, including the local curvature in relation to the overall surface geometry or the density of construction planes needed according to the degree of curvature. This required a broadening of fitness criteria from a static ranking device to an evaluation tool that evolves within a feedback loop of form generation and external analysis.

In the experiment many generations of two interrelated curved surfaces were bred in an environment defined by attracting and repelling forces, and the evolved surfaces were analysed in other software packages. Emergent geometric patterns informed and changed the fitness criteria accordingly. Geometric features such as the regional change in curvature and the direction of surface normals[6] defined the

position and number of construction planes, as well as the depth of the sections, across many populations. The guiding geometric relations were relatively simple, but through the nonlinear evolution intricate surface articulations were produced. Through the mutual adaptiogenesis of geometric fitness criteria and geometric articulation the morphogenetic process yielded an ever-increasing complexity, which always maintained the logic of the material system ready for immediate manufacturing with the laser cutter. The result of this experiment shows a level of complexity and coherence that is very difficult to achieve in conventional design approaches.

The second morphogenetic experiment, a design commission for a pneumatic strawberry bar for the Architectural Association's annual project review, went a step further. The main aim of this research project was to extend the evolutionary dynamics of reproduction, mutation, competition and selection as design strategies. The potentials and limits from initial form generation to the actual manufacturing process were explored by shifting the investigation towards performative patterns that evolve as species across populations and successive generations whilst maintaining structural capacity and geometric characteristics.

The logic of a pneumatic component is defined by the geometry of its cutting pattern, and this was the starting point of the Genr8-driven development process. The pneumatic component of the experiment consisted of two trapeziform surfaces that are aligned at a datum, the plane of the connecting seams. The inflated component is a 3-D form defined by the different lengths of the surfaces in relation to the defining points and the spatial datum. These simple geometric relations, defined as a generic 3-D cutting-pattern,

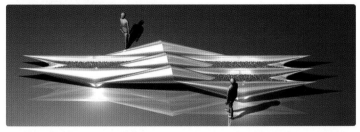

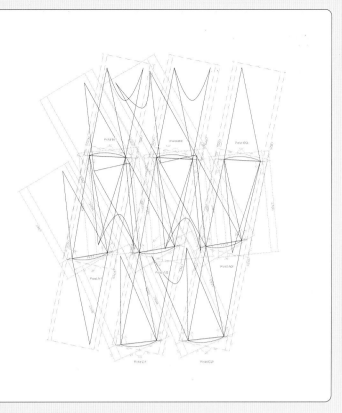

Opposite, top left
Morphogenetic design: a generation of three surface subpopulations grown in Genr8 provides the geometric definition points for different component structures. This population consists of 'individual' pneumatic systems that are all coherent with the relevant structural and manufacturing logics.

Opposite, top right
After running a digital evolutionary process in Genr8 over 600 generations, 144 species were identified and catalogued according to specific patterns of relevant geometric features. The taxonomy is related to the surface definition ('S' on y-axis) and the component layout ('C' on x-axis).

Above, top and middle left
The digital model of the individual to be manufactured shows the differentiation of the pneumatic components within the self-supporting overall system.

Above, bottom left
A prototype manufactured from clear PVC indicates that the evolving differentiation of each component is still coherent with the relevant structural and manufacturing logics.

Above right
Digitally derived 3-D cutting-pattern.

provided the base data for the subsequent process that simultaneously grew three subpopulations of surfaces. Two subpopulations evolved the definition points of the shorter and the longer surfaces, and one defined the spatial datum. According to the logic of the pneumatic base, component-specific fitness criteria for each subpopulation of the geometry-defining surfaces were established, which influenced the global undulation and surface subdivision in relation to parametric variables such as the scale factor of growth, branch length and branch angles.

The evolving points of local maximum distances between the shorter and the longer surfaces in relation to the datum surface established the definition points of the pneumatic system. Rather than breeding just one surface, this method instigated a feedback loop by continuously using the bounding box of the most recently evolved surface as the environment in which the next surface would be grown. This method maintained the inherent logic of the pneumatic component in a larger system but dissolved the distinction between environmental constraints and individual response. Another feedback loop utilised digital form finding in a dedicated membrane engineering software, and additional physical test-modelling further informed the evolutionary process and its evaluation.

After running Genr8 over 600 generations, 144 species were identified and catalogued according to specific patterns of relevant geometric features. Considering the interrelated evolution of the geometry-defining surfaces,

the criterion for evaluation was the relative fitness amongst the emergent species rather than the absolute fitness ranking of any particular individuals. As the structural behaviour of the pneumatic system primarily relied on specific geometric relations such as alignment and proportional distances of definition points, the species of individuals that shared these geometric features was selected. The individual of the chosen species that grew in the last and most developed generation was then selected. The genotype of this individual incorporated the genomes of three geometry-defining surfaces, establishing a degree of phenotypic plasticity that allowed the resulting pneumatic system to adjust to the constraints of a digital cutting-pattern and computer-aided manufacturing process.

The two morphogenetic experiments described above indicate the power of evolutionary computation as a design tool that can produce intricate surface articulations that are coherent within the geometric logic of the relevant material and structural system. This is the beginning of a convergence of the digital tools developed in recent years, in which genetic and generative algorithms play a key role. Once complex modelling and evaluation techniques such as finite element analysis and fluid dynamics can be merged with evolutionary computation, an unknown level of design complexity and truly integrated design and manufacturing will be achievable. This suggests a new intellectual framework, one in which the focus of design is not a singular finished product but the recognition of operative patterns, the taxonomy of performative species and the detection of emergent phenomena embedded in an inclusive evolutionary process. Genr8 allows us to glimpse into this future of evolutionary architecture. ⌂

Drunk in an Orgy of Technology

Professor Chris Wise is director of expedition engineering and chair of civil engineering design at Imperial College, London. He is an eminent design engineer and external examiner to the Emergent Technologies and Design masters programme at the AA. Here he reflects on intoxication with technology, mathematics and computers, and with emergence.

Technology and beer … are they by any chance related? In the 'emergent' world I think they might be. Here comes a generation drunk on technology – using it to get rid of a few of those old-world inhibitions and venture into hyperspace to play with things their grandmothers wouldn't dream of. Escapist stuff from the world of PS2. When I was student I used to get a similar effect by cranking up the feedback on my electric guitar – until something strange happened and I got a hangover, totally rebelled against the unstoppability of it all and just wanted to sit under a tree. After a few hours on a computer I get the same feeling – what begins as liberation becomes ponderous, too predictable, too heavy.

'Apparently the word 'technology' comes from old Greek and means 'the systematic treatment of an art'. Here 'art' means skill. Our interest also lies in the words 'system' (it can be made into an algorithm) and 'treatment' (it can be manipulated). So it is inevitable that as a new technological 'system' emerges, so does new art, or even architecture. It emerges, comes into the world and fights for survival. Within this algorithm the system designer is all-powerful, outside of it he is all weakness, unless he has a very broad skill base.'

If I look at our engineering students, it is rare to find one whose skill set embraces both analysis and synthesis. Elsewhere some, like the sculptor John Pickering, use equations as the skeleton on which they hang their work, but during the design process quite deliberately intervene to give the outcome a shape they like. In Pickering's case, he links the algorithms to his love of life drawing. Then he builds fairly rough 3-D cardboard jigs to hold the gossamer-pure mathematics.

Many more, including myself if I'm honest, are less interested in the maths than the answers. We like to look for patterns, forms, for an underlying structure. And even if we don't quite understand all of the equations, we can gasp at the beauty of the answers. Probably this is a learned response, looking for something familiar, some cute elegance. I recently saw the mathematician Marcus du Sautoy gradually add together lots of harmonics to get every single prime number from one to infinity. It had the air of a conjuring trick. No doubt he'd worked out a defined process, using a very clever algorithm that was beyond me. But it seemed like magic. He managed to explain in the language not of maths, but of music, one of the unfathomable mysteries of the universe. You just had to say 'Wow! How does nature do that?' or, simply, 'Why?'.

How does a whiff of 'emergent technology' add to this great body of human achievement? The very name hints at the creature from the black lagoon. The answer is in the hands of the practitioners, those very clever people who are currently exploring the world of genetic algorithms and their applications.

Is technology the fountainhead of their design? For some it certainly is their drug of choice. But, so far, emergent technology themes evolve painstakingly slowly, hindered by the limitations of the very systems of software and rapid manufacture that opened the door in the first place. We can be glad of the patience of these pioneers, and very optimistic for them as their tools get faster. Maybe soon the technology will grow to define both the system and the treatment of the resulting art – learning from itself, and even from outside the algorithm completely. Imagine if such a process could dip into humanity when it needed inspiration, not vice versa.

Unlike life, in a computer everything is number perfect. It is fascinating to see what the students of the AA's newly emerging MA/MArch programme are coming up with – their version of the artistic approach is to use a device, or a piece of software, see where it goes seemingly of its own volition and respond accordingly. This is great, as they will definitely be taken into worlds they hadn't even thought could exist. But it begs the question of who is driving whom? The computer doesn't seek familiar answers but follows only the rules set for it by the students. As if nature hadn't given them enough to study, so they want to find more, and then invent theories and maxims to use what they find.

If I had a criticism it seems that the systems are more sophisticated than the way they are being used, their full potential as yet unrealised. So I would like to see a more proactive approach initially, with the systems more grounded, certainly more physical. To be able to kick these things around, to bring a nonrational but human brain to bear. I would want to be able to do some shaping anywhere along the road. In short I would want it to be interactive and instant. I don't want a fancy computer program that ends up turning our base metal into gold and back again before we've even realised it.

Along with power comes responsibility – even with today's 'fab' computers we are utopia-bytes short of enough computing power to study what we really want to study, so the computer goes along a very narrow path. It only stops when it's told to. Mimicking Darwin, computerised mutations jump the process into another groove in the hope that somehow the fittest will survive. But the definition of 'fitness' is usually arbitrary, so the tools stunt their own creativity.

Some exceptionally gifted people, like the late engineer Peter Rice, habitually link technology, and especially maths, back to their minds to help them converge on an essential design truth, to distil a pure answer. Often this gave Rice a very strong diagram, a robust core. But even he said: 'I'm a bit like a hound following a fox; I'm following something really close to the ground and I can't actually see where it's going.' He might have chosen the chicken and the egg instead.

So far, the emerging technologist has usually had to limit the output of the process to an object rather than a project. A project has a definite purpose. A project has a site. A project interacts with people. It interacts with climate. It interacts with time. And unlike a computer process it is made of imperfect materials and things that change according to this interaction. In short, the project lives. And in part, in having a life, it enriches the lives of those involved in putting together the project and the next one. Somehow the algorithm and the wax modeller don't quite do this for me. Yet.

Is emergent technology investigation or creation? Do these processes start with us or finish with us? Today we see emergent phenomena without knowing whether they are in the mainstream or up a sideline. The next generation of these emergent tools should make us a wonderful alternative world of things that no one ever imagined could exist, but whether they work depends on the boundaries set by the system designer. Choosing the rules, acting as judge and jury – probably this is where we have the biggest development challenge. Because we can make new things, our aspirations for what we can have, what we can afford, what we know will work, will change. This is marvellous, an eye-opening process that should be nurtured. However, the key to the success of the whole caboodle is the human mind which, like Peter Rice, filters, edits, composes, interrogates and challenges.

So I would like to advocate less algorithms, more responsiveness, less technological drunkenness and more direction. Less silicone-chippery, more brain. But I can't quite do it.

I do actually think that a massive technological orgy will happen anyway and might get us further, faster, even if it has the directional stability of a bucking bronco.

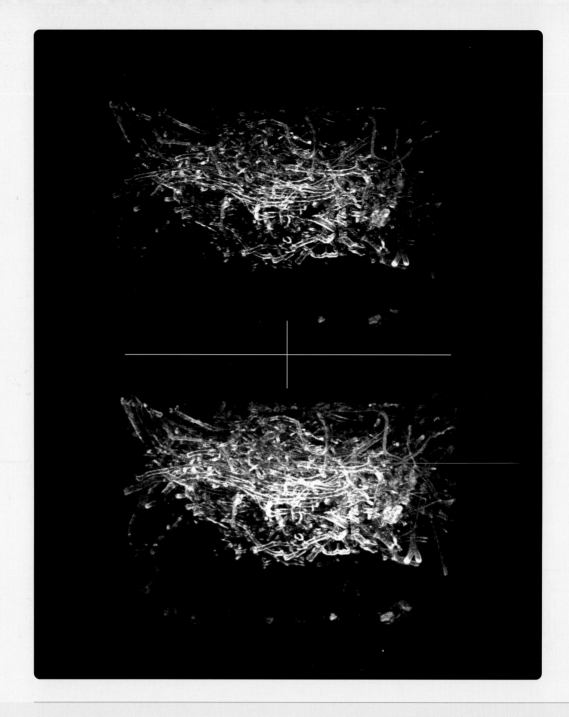

Emergent Technologies
and Design

MA Dissertation Project

Data-Graphics and
Continuous Datasets:
Digital Imaging, Mapping
and Modelling
of Complex Material
Systems

Lina Martinson

The digital imaging, mapping and modelling of a complex
structure such as a bird's nest demonstrates the capacity
and limits of available digital technologies while revealing
the fact that these tools as yet do not belong to the tool-set
of architectural design. With a growing number of
architectural projects based on complex morphological
articulation it becomes increasingly necessary to introduce
available state-of-the-art technologies from other
disciplines and develop these for combined architectural
and engineering purposes.

The available choice of technologies expands the potential
of the 'continuous data set' by enabling descriptions at
multiple resolution levels and allowing seamless transitions
between differing 'description types'. For example, a graphic
information entity can be transformed into a morphometric
description. The ability to constantly move between, and
integrate, differing descriptive methods introduces a powerful
tool for analysis and design.

Descriptive conventions exist within all disciplines, each
employing different techniques, data types and processes.
Any descriptive technique and representation 'type'
inherently defines the boundaries for analysis and design.
Frequently, the data type employed within any particular
discipline is not compatible with data types in other

disciplines. Within the earth sciences and medical disciplines the
treatment of information is graphic, employing pattern recognition to
decipher spatial features of interest, to search for valuable natural
resources or the occurrence of pathological conditions. The data sets
are made up of voxel units, volume elements that are essentially
3-D pixels. The initial definition of data resolution may vary from
micrometre to kilometre, producing immense files that require
extensive processing. In order to manage these vast spatial data
bases, a range of different methods for postprocessing of the data
is employed in mapping and modelling a bird's nest, allowing for
measurements and analysis of the material.

In contrast, the representation type in common use in architecture
is the vector, point coordinates expressed as NURBS or polygons
depending on modelling platform. The limitations of the respective
data types are evident. Vector data is highly convertible, easily
movable through most architectural modelling programs, and the
data set is small enough to use in off-the-shelf components. Voxel
data is highly specialised, the depth of information requires a much
higher processing capacity, and heavily customised software is
required in order to realise its full potential. The voxel is properly
defined as a 'fluid' information entity. Its usage encompasses
multiple resolution levels, the merging of interior and exterior
definitions, and it may be converted from graphic volume to
coordinate surface description. The 'fluid' character of the voxel data

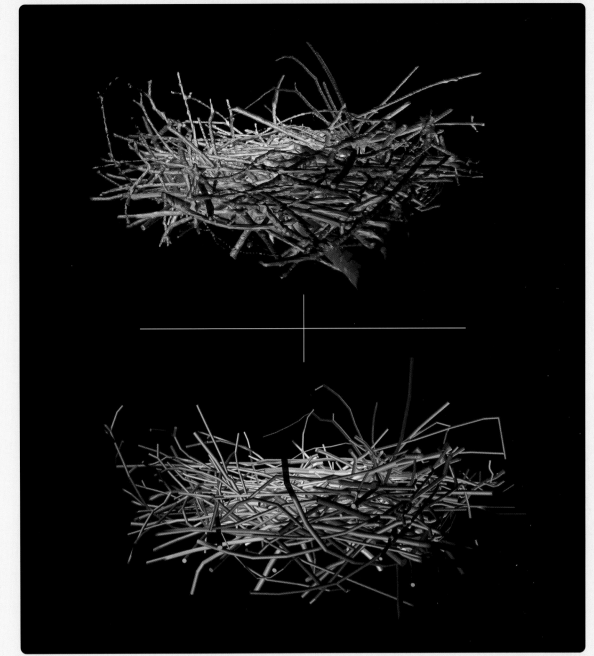

is employed within medical-imaging sciences to switch
between visualising conditions related to shape and spatial
definitions of the location of phenomena. In addition, it
enables the definition of internal systems by varying the
definition of 'internal' and 'external' shape. Data
management is crucial if voxel data is to be usable for
architectural analysis and design. Decreasing the immense
size of the voxel file by converting it into a surface mesh
drastically improves the abilities for further processing and
rendering of the 3-D image data in cross-platform
applications.

This suggests a preliminary formulation for a spatial data
base. Voxel data is produced through exposing the study
object to an external influence, such as radio waves,
magnetic energy or radiation. The signal reflected back by
the material of the object is recorded. The resulting map
describes the gradients of signal intensity produced by
varying material properties, visualised as differentiated
brightness levels in the volume of the 3-D image. The
researcher interacts with the data through defining
'visualisation limits', the signal intensity levels of interest for
the analysis. This is a pure graphic treatment of information.
Thereafter, the data may be postprocessed through
performing calculations of the material, quantifying and

identifying the occurrence of various material properties. This record
of variable 'field conditions' is convertible and allows the
transformation from a data type that describes image volume to
a triangulated surface mesh description. Depending on the initial
parameters of the calculation, defining the range of maximum to
minimum signal intensity levels that are to be measured, the resulting
mesh is reproduced in outline or in detail. There may need to be a
balance sought between processing-intense data volume and potential
loss of data for use in computationally inferior environments. This
suggests that there is a constant negotiation between defining the
boundaries for analysis and ensuring an achievable result.

In this research the voxel data set was processed using an algorithm
known as 'marching cubes'. The algorithm works by subdividing 3-D
space into a series of small cubes. The algorithm then 'moves' through
each of the cubes, tests the corner points and replaces the cubes with
an appropriate set of polygons. The sum total of all polygons generated
will be a surface that approximates the one the voxel data set describes.
The volume data was thus converted into a single continuous
triangulated surface. Further data management was produced through
subsampling, which helped reduce the file size sufficiently. From the
Visualisation Tool Kit format, the data was exported into a file format
that provides compatibility for import into an off-the-shelf polygon-
based 3-D modelling program where further formal and structural
analysis and manipulation of the bird's nest was carried out.

Adaptable Equilibrium
Elastic Behaviour and
Dynamic Adaptability

Wolf Mangelsdorf,
Buro Happold

The processes by which natural systems maintain their continuity, their adaptation to changes in their environment, have been the focus of intense study in the sciences of emergence. Following is an examination of the potential for achieving the adaptable structures by the architectural engineering of elastic behaviour, and the role of equilibrium in controlling the dynamics of designed movements.

Although we might not be aware of it, elasticity is everywhere around us. We hardly feel how the materials that we sit on, stand on or walk on deform under the influence of the external forces they are exposed to or, once these forces no longer act, how they return to their undeformed state. Living things achieve very high strength and elastic behaviour with soft and extendable tissues, and are able to carry loads and grow. Soft natural tissues are very strong, and achieve flexibility and adaptability with simple fibre members, arranged in complex hierarchies. One potent way of approaching the design and production of adaptable structures is to examine the characteristics of elastic material behaviour.

Elasticity is one of the most important characteristics of the physical world, and is the result of the chemical bonds between the atoms that a material is made of. One can imagine them as springs between atoms, holding them together and at the same time reacting to any forces that act on them. In traditional engineering terms, elasticity is defined as the deformation in relation to a stress in a material. Different materials have different elasticity, for example the elasticity of rubber can be felt when you stretch it in your hand. A steel band of the same shape and proportions feels very stiff, but it, too, has elasticity. A force of about a thousand times more than you apply to a rubber band is needed to achieve the same effect.

In most cases we relate to elasticity as degrees of stiffness. And although both elastic and stiff describe the same material property we usually associate elastic with weak, and stiff with strong. This is a common misconception because stiffness describes only the deflection of a material under stress. We think of the strength of a material as the limit of the material to withstand stresses elastically, and once stresses go beyond this limit a material will deform irreversibly. This phenomenon is called plastic deformation. The results are then dependent on the material, so that most metals will show a plastic deformation and therefore a slow and controllable failure. Glass, however, lacks the ability for plastic deformation, so its failure is brittle and explosive.

Besides the elasticity of the material, though, another important factor influences the behaviour of structures: the profile of its members. In the physical equation elastic strain is expressed in reference to material stresses or, more simply, to the cross-sectional area of material to which a force is applied. This is easily understood using the example of a rubber band to which we apply tension: its axial stiffness determines its elongation under the pulling force. The thicker the band, the more force is needed to elongate the band. The greater cross-sectional area increases its axial stiffness. In the case of bending, the definition of cross-sectional stiffness is somewhat more complex, but becomes clear when we look in more detail at what happens in a structural element. Caused by offset external forces, bending moments will have to be resisted by a coupling of tension and compression forces within the member, creating a resistance of equal magnitude. The part of a cross section under tension will be elongated, that under compression will be shortened. The member bends about a neutral axis, a line that flexes but does not undergo any elongation or shortening.

The amount of material in a cross section resisting compression, and that resisting the tension on the opposite side of the neutral axis, define the bending stiffness of a structural element. This is described in a geometrical value, the moment of inertia. It varies for different types of cross section, as the influence of material grows with its quadratic distance from the neutral axis. It becomes obvious that as a result the stiffness of a beam increases in relation to its depth. With the flexure and the resulting elongation and shortening, stresses are created within the material, which again depend on its elasticity. A less stiff member is flexed more easily and stresses created out of this flexure are lower than those in a stiffer member. Higher stiffness will result in higher stresses under a similar bending, so much so that a stiffer member might be stressed to its limit strength and fail before reaching the otherwise largest possible deformation. Stiff is not always better.

Splitting the forces into tension and compression within a member has direct implications on its stiffness, stresses and deflection. This is true for all structures – taking forces in bending will always require more material than if the forces are taken axially. However, structures that are acting in pure axial forces or only in bending are rare. A superimposition of both creates an interaction and an influence on stiffness, as stresses and resulting strains are added. This becomes particularly interesting in surface structures, where curvature and in-plane reactions are utilised, and bending stiffness is provided at the same time. Utilising the two parameters provides a subtle way to generate the necessary stiffness in a structure, using many small members rather than few large ones. Connections between members control their interactions and allow stiffness as well as strength to be added where necessary or when required. Stiffness can be reduced where it is superfluous, while flexibility can be introduced as and where desired.

This strategy is applied in the design of fibre composites, where strength and stiffness are supplied where needed by the fibre layout. The matrix design ensures the interaction of the fibres and their integration into the higher geometrical order of the structural component. It is also found in many natural structures. Additional manipulation of the cross section of individual members, either by varying thickness or varying section geometry, will produce varying stiffness, which can be deployed differently in different directions. Used in combination, these principles will achieve adaptability in structural systems. Deformation and flexibility will not contradict elastic stiffness and limitation of deformation under primary loading conditions. As axial stiffness is in general greater than bending stiffness, it follows that stiffness is most easily provided using surface and shape, increasing the amount of forces carried in the plane of the structure. Bending capacity becomes a secondary action and introduces a means of control and of positive deformation. The addition of elements, each with a smaller stiffness, allows the stiffness allocation of the structure to be designed. Connection of single elements can increase axial stiffness but can also be utilised in bending, as outer forces can be split into tension and compression in the structural macro arrangement.

There is, however, a complication that needs to be taken into account. Whilst tension forces are inherently stabilising as they pull and elongate a structural element, compression forces create a very different effect. The material, right down to the atomic level, tries to evade compressive forces, by moving out of the line of action. On a macro level this creates a stability problem, the buckling under a critical axial load, which results in the flexure of the member. The same phenomenon applies also to bent elements. As moments are creating internal tension and compression, the compressive part will show a reaction similar to that of a strut under axial load. It will try to move out of the line of force, but is restrained from doing so by the tying forces in the tensile part of the cross section. In these circumstances the only available movement is a sideways twist and rotation, known in engineering terms as lateral torsional buckling.

In the simpler case of pure compression the flexure created by the buckling will create an offset of forces and inner resistance. The resulting moment is added to the compression force so that there is now more need for strength and stiffness, not only in axial compression but also in bending. The increase of the stresses within the member will lead to increasingly greater deformations, which in turn have a detrimental effect on the member's ability to carry loads, and weakness is increased. The stability of axially loaded members is directly related to their bending stiffness.

The context in which these forces act on individual members is the global structural arrangement, and equilibrium is needed for its stability. In order to avoid acceleration and movement, any force acting in the structure has to be reacted to by a force of opposite direction and equal magnitude. Finding equilibrium at a minimum level of potential energy is one of the basic principles in nature and physics. The behaviour of a soap bubble is a good example. A sphere is the smallest surface to enclose any given volume, so the equilibrium of internal pressure and tension in the soap film will always create a spherical bubble. It can be thought of as the minimum energy surface specific to the particular boundary constraints in action at the time.

Similar ideas can be applied when designing structures. Tension structures show this behaviour in the most pronounced way, as they change their geometry to find the minimum energy geometry. Although not so directly visible, the principle can also be found at work in other structures. If more than one load path is theoretically possible, it will always be the one with the lowest possible level of potential energy. It

follows that more than one equilibrium state can be achieved within a structure, as long as there are different modes and levels of resistance. Changing the arrangement of external forces and reactions, and altering the boundary conditions will make the structure change from one equilibrium state to another. Where external forces are not directly resisted by reaction the potential energy will be transformed into kinetic energy, with resulting movements. These transitions must be designed, and a stable static equilibrium state provided for each end of the transition. If the transition increases the energy in the whole structure, both the equilibrium states will be of a lower energy level and therefore more stabile. It is not the transition that is the problem but the control, which can be achieved through the manipulation of boundary conditions and active changes to geometry.

Adaptability and controlled dynamics of structures are part of the new concepts of structure that are emerging. The arrangement of members and material in a structure can allow us to manipulate stiffness as well as strength. This can be achieved in various ways, such as the orientation of members, or by fibre additions on either micro or macro levels, or by the control of the interaction between members. However, this is to be related to the global geometry and global structural behaviour. The intelligent combination of bending and axial action allows us to utilise the much higher axial stiffness, and we can design the member arrangements so that bending flexibility can enable adaptability and controlled dynamics. The geometry of the structure will play a most important role in this deployment of forces and stiffness, creating the need for surfaces to be structurally designed and integrated into combinatorial load paths.

Sufficient built-in redundancy of members is an essential characteristic for adaptability, and the provision of a multitude of load paths can assist the transition stages of dynamic adaptation. Transitions can be induced in the structure by the designed application of external forces, by mechanical devices or the simple adjustment of the boundary conditions.

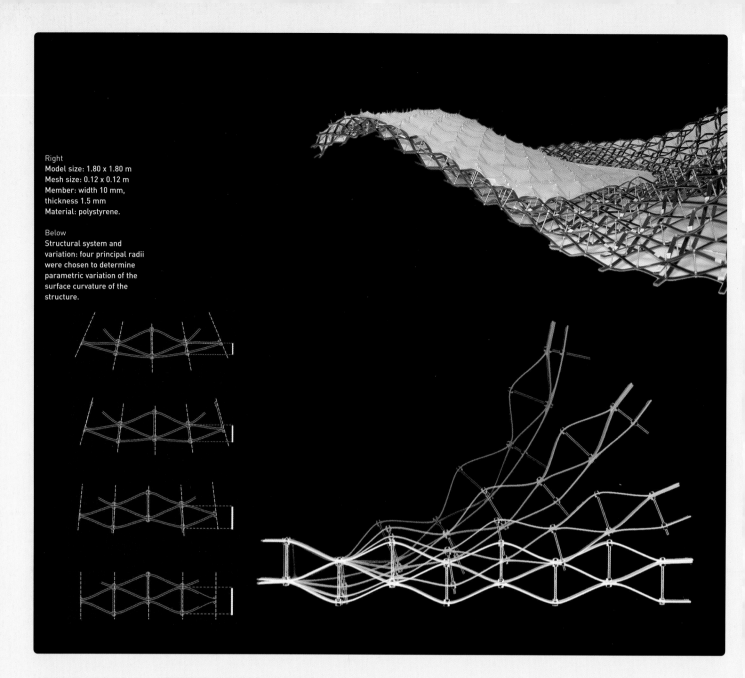

Right
Model size: 1.80 x 1.80 m
Mesh size: 0.12 x 0.12 m
Member: width 10 mm,
thickness 1.5 mm
Material: polystyrene.

Below
Structural system and
variation: four principal radii
were chosen to determine
parametric variation of the
surface curvature of the
structure.

Emergent Technologies
and Design

MA Dissertation Project

HybGrid: Form Generation
and Form Finding of
Adaptable Structures

Sylvia Felipe and
Jordi Truco

HybGrid is an MA dissertation project aimed at making grid-shell structures adaptable. The project fuses grid shell with space-frame logic. A layered grid-shell with uniform grid layout made from elastic members becomes globally defined through local manipulations of actuators that regulate the distance between the members of the layered lattices. Evolving a form with the capacity for multiple equilibrium configurations involved the use of genetic algorithms and material experiments, linking changing spatial requirements to their corresponding formal and structural articulation.

The physical articulation was based on the property of elastic deformation. In natural structures this kind of deformation increases the shaping possibilities in a simple and economical way, and maintains the endurance properties that are characteristic of material continuity. The HybGrid follows these principles by utilising the elastic properties of materials such as polymers and fibre composites. Fibre composites have an extremely optimised elastic/resistance capacity. The system is based on a grid made up of fibre-composite strips. These strips are continuous and preshaped in order to achieve the required inertia without unnecessary stressing of the material. The production method is quite simple, as there is no need for differentiation in the configuration of the grid during the production process. The system can later generate formal and structural differentiation by changing the relative distances between these strips. These distances are easily changed by

the use of actuators placed between layered strips. Each activator has four possible positions that define the distances between strips.

Varying programmatic and spatial requirements are transferred to the design by means of parametric control through the software written for this purpose. The design of the system implies the design of the software, so that the limits, rules and ranges of the system are parametrically defined in relation to the maximum and minimum curvature radii at local and global levels. The software can respond to desired changes in the global configuration, the size and location of required internal spaces. Once these spaces are digitally defined, the software calculates the required local position to each 'actuator', which will have a unique address. The system is able to adapt to multiple requirements while operating on simple rules organised by an algorithm based on the combination of the four positions or radii. The actual form of the artefact is therefore not the product of the personal and unidirectional view of the architect, but is produced by a collaborative process, which continues to affect changes to the form in use.

There is no dichotomy between form finding and adaptation of the form in use, as form finding continues each time a change to the building is activated. This extends the idea of form finding from shape optimisation for a single minimum-energy configuration under stress into a dynamic structural system. It combines multiple configurations or equilibrium states in a structural system with a control system that produces complex global transitions between forms from very simple local rules. A full-scale construction was built at the Architectural Association School of Architecture in July 2003. ⚿

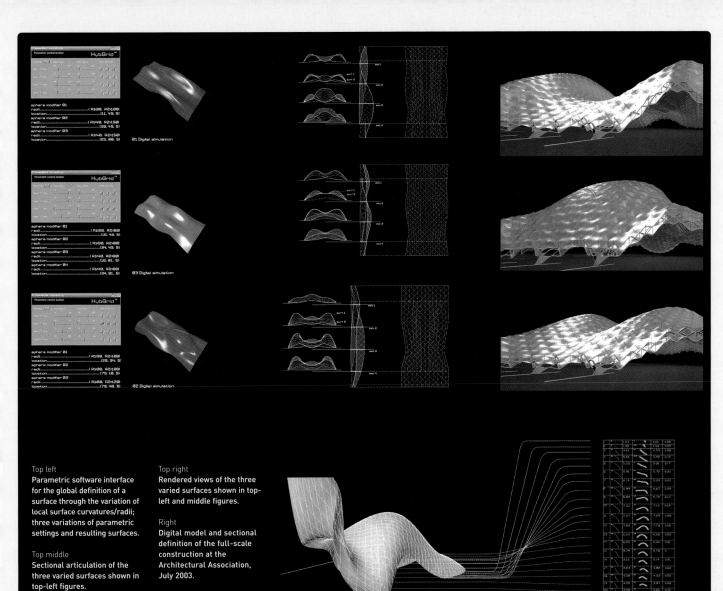

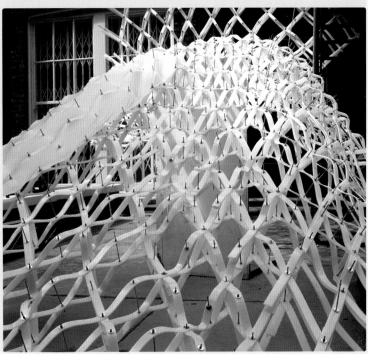

Top left
Parametric software interface for the global definition of a surface through the variation of local surface curvatures/radii; three variations of parametric settings and resulting surfaces.

Top middle
Sectional articulation of the three varied surfaces shown in top-left figures.

Top right
Rendered views of the three varied surfaces shown in top-left and middle figures.

Right
Digital model and sectional definition of the full-scale construction at the Architectural Association, July 2003.

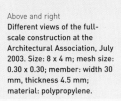

Above and right
Different views of the full-scale construction at the Architectural Association, July 2003. Size: 8 x 4 m; mesh size: 0.30 x 0.30; member: width 30 mm, thickness 4.5 mm; material: polypropylene.

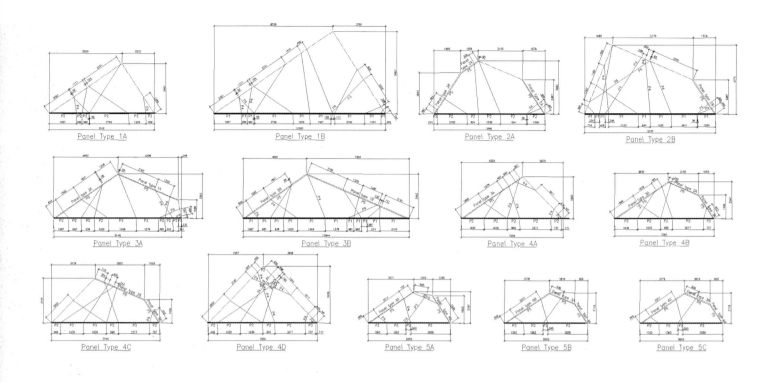

Panel Type 1A Panel Type 1B Panel Type 2A Panel Type 2B

Panel Type 3A Panel Type 3B Panel Type 4A Panel Type 4B

Panel Type 4C Panel Type 4D Panel Type 5A Panel Type 5B Panel Type 5C

Engineering Design:
Working with Advanced
Geometries

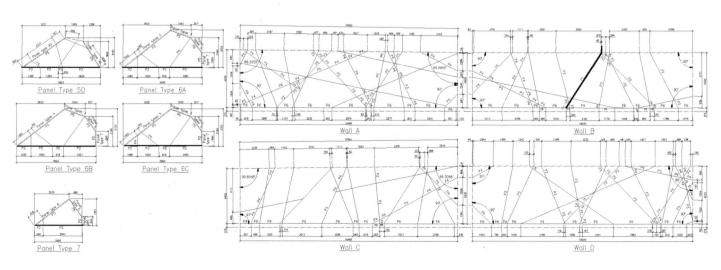

Panel Type 5D Panel Type 6A

Panel Type 6B Panel Type 6C

Panel Type 7

Wall A Wall B

Wall C Wall D

In conversation with the **Emergence and Design Group**, Charles Walker, leader of the Advanced Geometry Unit (AGU) at **Arup & Partners**, discusses the unit's multidisciplinary way of integrating architectural design with engineering. As well as its involvement in many other projects, AGU has worked with Toyo Ito on the Serpentine Gallery Summer Pavilions in 2002, with Anish Kapoor for the Marsyas sculpture of the Unilever series at Tate Modern, and David Adjaye on the British Pavilion at the Venice Biennale 2003. Each of these structures involved a unique and complex exploration.

Toyo Ito, Serpentine Gallery Summer Pavilions, London, 2002
Opposite
Structural panels schedule drawing.

Above
Exterior view of the pavilion, designed by Toyo Ito in collaboration with Cecil Belmond.

The Advanced Geometry Unit (AGU) at Arup & Partners has an interesting composition, with an architect, three engineers, a mathematician and a scientist making up the small permanent team. Together they work on basic research and are connected to another 30 engineers working on specific projects in a wider network. All of the permanent members of the unit have multidisciplinary backgrounds, combining engineering with architecture, mathematics, physics or computer programming. Leadership of the group is in the hands of Charles Walker, a chartered architect and a chartered engineer, who describes the scope of AGU's work and elaborates on its notion of advanced geometry.

'The Advanced Geometry Unit at Arup was set up for the purpose of research and design in geometrically complex form and structure. The mandate for AGU is to explore new organisational strategies based in the burgeoning field of new mathematics. The unit takes a specific interest in the use of algorithms, fractal mathematics and nonlinearity in structure. To achieve this end, new digital software for both computer modelling (parametric and relational) as well as structural analysis (using both finite element numerical modelling and other techniques such as dynamic relaxation) form the working tools for developing geometrically complex nonlinear design.

'Advanced Geometry was really a working title that stuck. By "advanced", we wish to concern ourselves with developments in new mathematics, for example

Chris Ofili and David Adjaye,
British Pavilion, 50th Venice
Biennale, 2003
Above
Chris Ofili's exhibition (with
David Adjaye) 'Within Reach'
at the British Pavilion for
the 50th Venice Biennale.
The glass ceiling is made of
176 coloured-glass panels in
the motif of a seven-pointed
star to create an immersive
environment to experience
the art.

Right
Close-up of the glass ceiling.

chaos theory, as opposed to Euclidean geometry. Our ambition is to break out of the Euclidean box or cage that structures much of our environment specifically through the use of new structural organisations. We are interested in a new paradigm, for example 3-D packing which is noncuboid, as the underlying organisational structure of architectural space.

'We use numerical models in structural analysis, which is to say numerical computer models. Our software can read in a DXF model, giving nodes and the connectivity matrix of a structure. We then assign material and structural properties to the members and define a loading. Based on the individual member stiffnesses and the connectivity matrix, the computer assembles a generalised stiffness matrix for the structure as a whole, which it inverts to find the generalised flexibility matrix. The loading matrix is then applied to the flexibility matrix to slave the deflections, and forces can be derived from this. This is what we call the finite element method and has been in use for over 20 years. So engineers have been modelling in the computer for as long as architects, although our models do tend to be more precise and disciplined than architectural models constructed for visualisation.

'We consider geometry beyond a simple structural performance. As engineers we, too, wish to create a contemporaneous design and we see our discipline as equally cultural. But more importantly structure has always been the dual of architectural space. One cannot exist without the other. I mean structure in the general

Right
A series of rapid prototype
models are made at each
design iteration to find the
appropriate glass-panel
configuration and form for the
glass ceiling.

sense of the term, that which provides order. We have always worked with the finite limits of technology. But today there is a gap between what can be built and what can be imagined. Digital technology has progressed so fast that what is built is more limited by the imagination than by technology. This is where we look for opportunity.'

The problems AGU tackles are all very different and have involved 3-D bracing of interlocking planes, algorithms as a generative tool, the buckling stability of flat plates and the manipulation of stressed skins to achieve sculptural form. The fact that each project brings new problems requires the unit to develop a new approach for each design. Walker is very evidently excited by this, and about the methods, tools and techniques of AGU's work.

'Generally the problems we seek to solve are unique. On the basis of the design problem we form a project team, that is to say we assemble skill-sets specific to the design, on a project-by-project basis. This might involve a degree of computer modelling to solve the setting out, or the need to develop a new tool for the modelling that is not available, or the development of software to accommodate a new form-finding technique. As we face the problem, we begin to get a feeling for the specific skills that might be needed. We collect the appropriate individuals and "charette" the problem, encouraging the unusual, unconventional and extreme. Sometimes individuals drop away, to carry out other work, and new team members join. It's often very difficult to trace authorship in this process. We tend to own the designs collectively.

'Most of the methods we use are based on existing techniques, like finite element numerical analysis. However, in most of the projects there is often one aspect of the project that requires a new tool – either an auto-lisp routine needs to be written or sometimes something more sophisticated. For our research work

Chris Ofili and David Adjaye, British Pavilion, 50th Venice Biennale, 2003
Below
Section of space-frame with glass-panel positions.

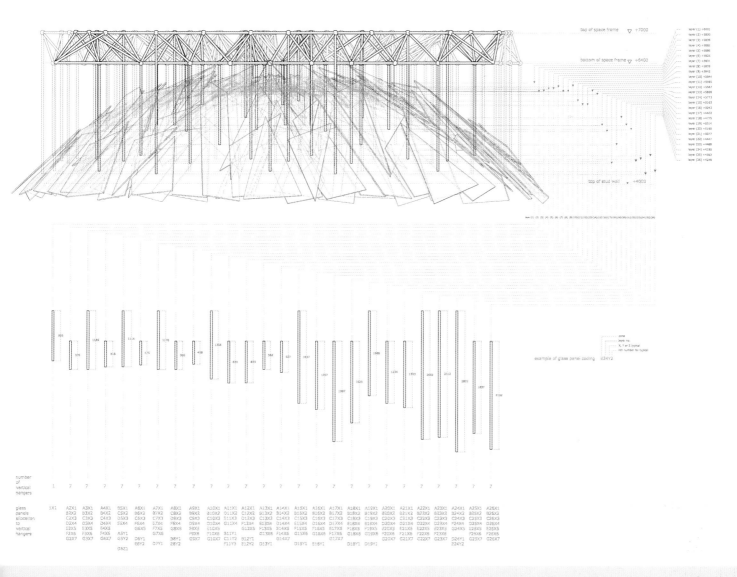

on Marsyas, a large sculpture with Anish Kapoor, Tristan Simmonds modified Fablon, our form-finding software, to form-find with inflation pressure applied to the elements. We don't do this sort of thing very often but making your own tools is definitely a higher form of craftsmanship.

'Our methods are very specific and as such no standard technique can develop. As an engineer I am quite focused on the project deliverables, or delivering the project. I'm not overly concerned about how we get there. Occasionally, when modelling a repetitive structure, the old-fashioned way of point-and-click over and over again is the most immediate. On other occasions we write a software patch to automate this. Usually we work with some fairly simple but reliable and effective tools. I'm not unhappy with this as it is the delivered project that interests me. Some of the guys in the group would like to develop our own tool box of wonder tools. I find each project so unique, and generally quite fast, that developing a wonder tool would be like hitting a moving target. I'm happy to use whatever is available at the time, even if it is not perfect, as long as it gets the job done. Occasionally we do pull old self-made tools out of the cupboard.'

The unusual composition of the team and the commitment to innovative tools for rapid development and delivery suggest a contemporary form of the atelier. It suggests that small independent practices, if sufficiently multidisciplinary, can successfully tackle very complex projects. The role of data and modelling in this environment is crucial, and a high degree of skill is required to work with, and modify, several different software packages.

'In many ways the way we work is similar to that of a small office. The key is to work very intensively in a small group and move quickly to a resolved design. The team members have to be passionate about what they are doing. They have to "buy in" intellectually and own the project or a specific part of it. The project succeeds on the strength of their efforts. It's the personal passion of the individual late at night that raises a project to a higher level. I don't place great value on where an idea comes from. It could be from the janitor or from my four-year-old son. It's recognising a good idea that I pride myself on, and when I see a twinkle in the eye of an engineer who will work all night to prove he is right, then I know we are getting somewhere. You don't need a big office for that.

'We use computer models first as initial visualisations or sketch models and then build more rigorous and robust working models. The analysis model develops out of these more rigorous studies.'

'We use many different commercial software packages for both modelling and analysis. For analysis we use Oasys (Ove Arup Systems) software as we have access to the code authors and can modify it if necessary. Tristan Simmonds is our code-meister when we need something different. Daniel Bosia often writes his own programs to develop geometry.

'Models play a big role in our work. We usually go straight to the computer. Physical models need to catch up. We use computer models first as initial visualisations or sketch models and then build more rigorous and robust working models. The analysis model develops out of these more rigorous studies. The data we use is generally structural analysis such that when an analysis is run we look at the hot spots and the performance generally, then make a proposal for improving the design and go back to the 3-D models to refine them. It's an iterative process.

'Our models are often very difficult to read, either printed or on screen. About three years ago we bought a solid printer, a ThermoJet from 3-D Systems. This has been fully integrated in our working method for some time and we often go very early to a solid wax model to test an idea. An automotive stylist once told me that you only get 40 per cent of the information about a surface on screen. This is because of parallax and the subtle nuances of natural light and motion that the machine can't replicate. It's absolutely true. Car stylists have known this, and this is why they still build clay slicks and reverse engineer their modifications. On the screen you simply can't get it right. On a recent project with artist Chris Ofili we stretched the limits of the solid modeller. It was a glass ceiling in Venice and without the wax models we couldn't have done it, that is, solve the collision detection and ensure it was what we wanted to build. But now I'm finding there is a scale problem. You can't get your head inside the wax models. I think the project would have been better if we had taken the model to a VR cave and stood inside it, then made a snagging list and reverse engineered the model. You only need this approach when you have some very complicated shapes in three dimensions. We had 176 angled planes of glass.

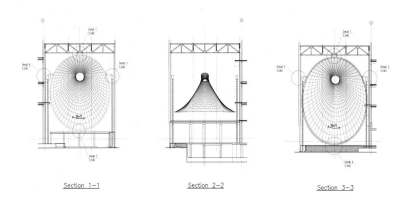

Section 1-1   Section 2-2   Section 3-3

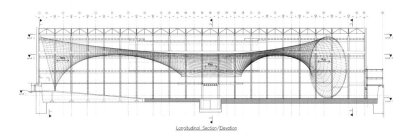

Longitudinal Section/Elevation

'Solid modelling is an integrated part of our work. We are not precious about these models. They are working tools that can easily be rebuilt. The important thing is having the machine right next to you in the office ready to go. It demystifies the process and allows you to play at first and discover the strengths and weaknesses of the medium. Actually it's rather dull and relatively simple to use. It still has limits. Often we get involved in building architectural models for competition entries, like a complicated curved space-frame roof with 10,000 elements. We use a bureau which builds in resin or nylon, and often send them much more complicated STL files than they ever get from the automotive industry.'

AGU is usually asked to collaborate in very complex and innovative structures. The role of the architect has to be quite different from that of the older convention, in which an architect brings a finished design to an engineer who acts as a consultant in a very strictly defined role. In innovative projects there is less concern with professional demarcation and more emphasis on the creative functioning of a network of contributors.

'We do tend to get involved from the very beginning of a project. This is usually because someone wants to do something new or speculative, but needs to know up

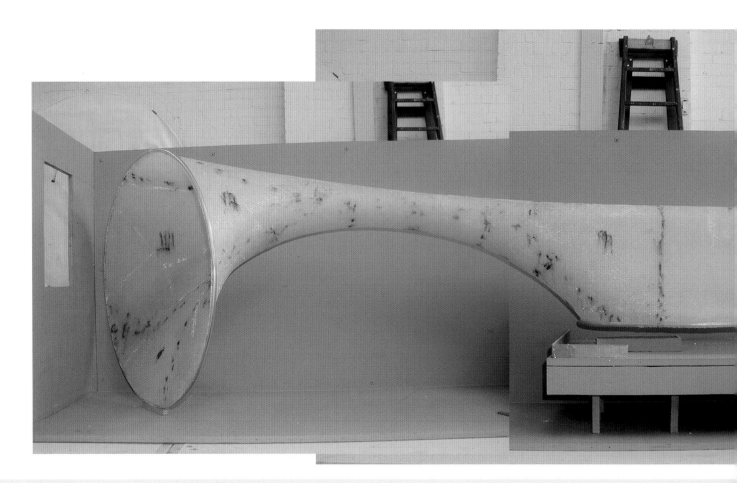

front what is and isn't possible. In this sense we become collaborators, often jointly authoring the design concept. If an architect is doing something he has done before, one knows the parameters. The engineering can come in later. But if you are looking for something unprecedented you need to work with first principles and you'll need an engineer there to agree. Even better, an engineer with a sparkle in his eye who will stay up all night to prove it works. It's all about intellectual "buy in". We're not very good at doing what we're told to do. We'll usually change something to make it our own.

'Increasingly, architects and clients are forming project teams in a similar manner to the way we resource projects internally, that is, assembling skill-sets on a project-by-project basis depending on the project needs. More and more we see networks of consultants coming together on a specific project then disbanding and reforming at another time for a different project. This departs from the traditional model where the client is at the top, with the architect next and the consultants below. In this new type of informal network both the client and the architect become two nodes within the diagram, but the centre of the project team could be the engineer. Similarly in, say, a bridge project, the engineer could have a closer link to the client than the architect. This eliminates the traditional control structure in favour of a network of specialists. Once this is established it no longer matters where one enters the network.

'A hundred years ago engineers worked for contractors. There was no consulting engineering profession. It's only since the modern movement and the stripping bare of structure that architects needed structural advice before tendering a project. In the last 50 years architects have deskilled and become very dependent on engineers. Today clients are experimenting with building procurement, trying to get the adversarial forces out of construction. Partnering is becoming common and people are beginning to take the longer-term view in their relationships with others. All of this encourages networking. I believe things will move in the direction of partnering and networking over the longer term. This could allow much greater creativity in design and construction, particularly as expertise from other fields, such as automotive and industrial design, are brought into the construction world.' ⌂

Anish Kapoor, Marsyas, Tate Modern, London, 2002
Opposite
Elevation and sections of Marsyas installation.

Below
Fibre-glass model of Marsyas installation.

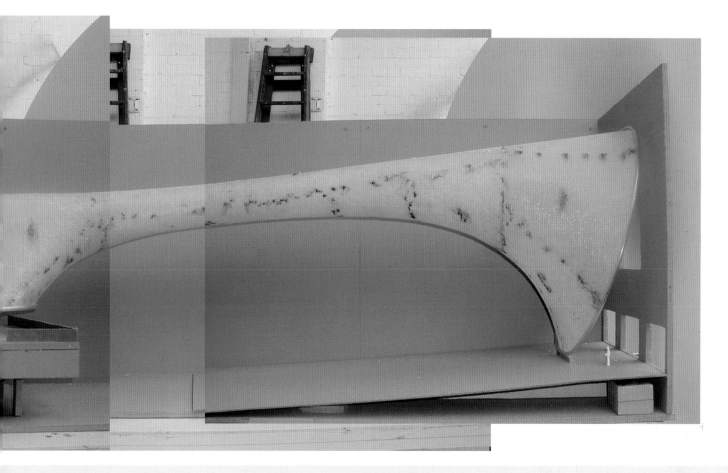

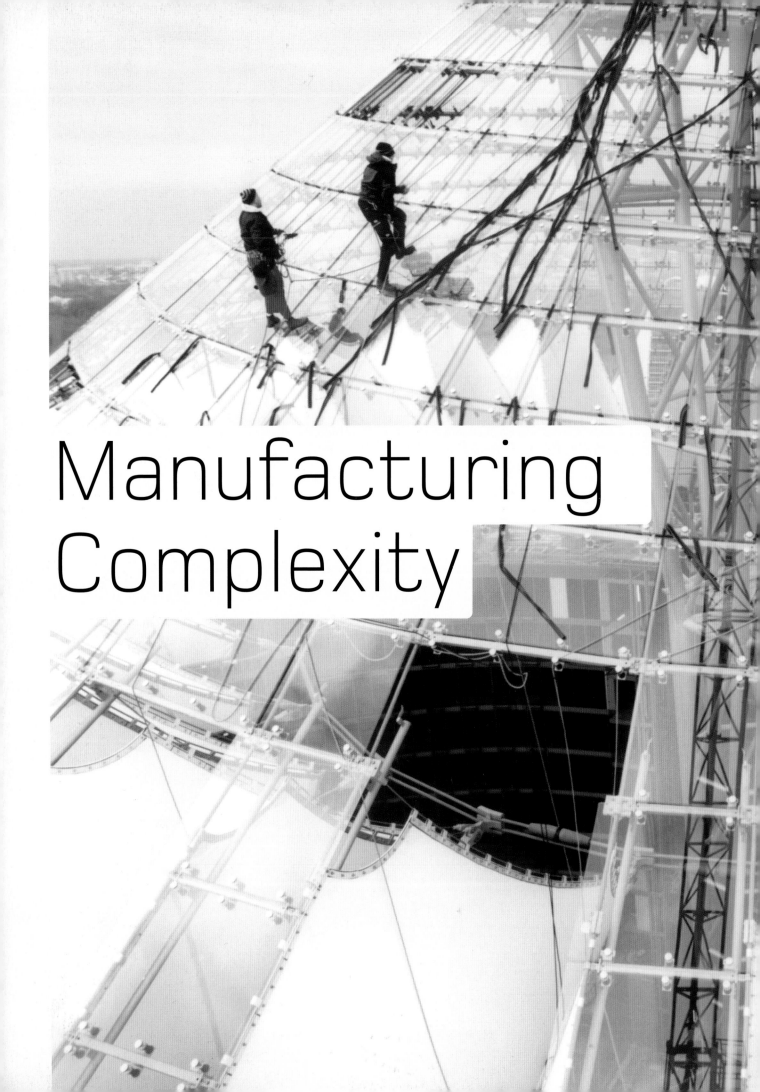

Manufacturing Complexity

Manufacturing contractor **Waagner Biro** is best known for complex geometry constructions. Managing director **Johann Sischka**, in conversation with the **Emergence and Design Group**, discusses the methods and construction strategies for complex structures such as the dome of the German Reichstag, the roof of the Great Court of the British Museum in London, and the roof of the Sony Center in Berlin.

Murphy/Jahn, Sony Center
Forum Roof, Berlin, 2000
Previous spread
Abseiling for the final
installation of the glass panels.

Waagner Biro has collaborated with distinguished architects including Foster & Parnters and Murphy/Jahn, as well as with the eminent engineering offices of Arup & Partners and Buro Happold. The challenges and problems encountered in the construction of complex geometry projects have driven a rethinking of conventional approaches to manufacturing and construction. With no architectural precedents to rely on, Waagner Biro had to develop a new construction rationale that could provide accuracy and stability for the manufacturing and assembly of Norman Foster's dome of the Reichstag.

'The biggest problem was the spiral ramp. This was the first really complex geometry project, as the curve has no constant radius and very little support, just a few pins on the outside of the ramp. We began to run two different computer systems simultaneously, each starting

from a different approach. All the steel plates that the ramp is made of are twisted, and with no constructed precedents it was not obvious what the best approach towards rationalising the geometry would be. Each section of the ramp was built up and variously precambered depending on the local support condition – we had to mark on the plate where the elements came together and then it was "folded back" for the flat plate to be cut.

'There was a very complex "stem" line, or organisational line, for the geometry of the ramp and the section of the ramp was also complex in form: it also had its own inclination within the ramp and the floor does not have a constant relation to the other pieces of the section. The question was how to put the ramp together in the most effective way? Fabricated jigs were set out to line up with the internal stiffeners of the ramp pieces, which were used for positive location. The coordinates of setting out were checked and pieces preassembled and tack-welded. Templates were used to match the ends of each assembled section to make sure that no kinks occur when the whole ramp is put together. The question of assembly was very

complex. A temporary structure was first built on site, and then the 18 pieces of the ramp were lifted into place and welded together until the whole ramp was complete. Next, the vertical members of the dome were put up and fixed to the temporary structure, and then the horizontals were put in place and welded to the verticals before the ramp was fixed to the completed dome structure. Finally the structure was "depropped" – the temporary structure was removed. The "proof" was the calculation of the completed structure, but the process of assembly had to be demonstrated to the proofing engineer.

'The moving sun-shading element added a further difficulty. When the components were manufactured and preassembled in the workshop, the individual sections looked very odd and to the human eye it was very difficult to see how they fitted together. The client, the site architect and ourselves were rather nervous about the possibility that the components might not fit together, but finally they did. We learned from this experience that a different sensibility is needed to be able to tell whether odd-looking pieces will eventually fit together.'

Preassembly of pieces of a structure on jigs does offer a positive location in controlled conditions, but the assembly of the whole of a complex geometry structure often requires a temporary structure. The Great Court roof for the British Museum is a steel lattice grid over a square plan. It is not completely symmetrical, and the behaviour during the construction process was rather complex, as grid-shells don't have any structural integrity until they are complete and in their final position.

'The roof is a steel grid-shell. In order to provide a geometric transition from the circular reading-room to the square courtyard-perimeter, Buro Happold deployed customised form-generating software to resolve architectural and structural requirements. The software generated two spirals winding in opposite directions to create a triangulated lattice. The transition from the short perimeter of the reading room to the longer one of the courtyard resulted in small triangles in the centre that progressively increase in size towards the outer perimeter. Prior to construction, a test piece was built to measure its deflection, in order to ensure that the structure would be both strong and sufficiently ductile. The key to its construction was a working platform on a 20-metre-high scaffold deck, where the construction took place and which had to hold up the weight of the roof during the assembly process. Our strategy was to allow complexity in only one element.

'To minimise potential difficulties in manufacturing and assembly we chose the members to be complex and the node to be simple. The 4,878 steel members that make up the grid-shell are therefore all different

Norman Foster, dome of the Reichstag, Berlin, 1999
Opposite, top
The complex assembly process of Norman Foster's dome of the Reichstag began with a temporary structure, which supported the 18 separate pieces of the ramp as they were welded together to make one continuous ramp.

Opposite, middle left
The ramp, which has a curve with no constant radius, is supported by only a few pins on the outside.

Opposite, middle right
Internal view from the ramp.

Opposite, bottom
Depropped dome. The completed ramp, with the vertical and horizontal dome members in place and the temporary structure removed.

Above
Checking of the complex geometry of the ramp was carried out on a jig, which aligned with the internal stiffeners of the ramp pieces, providing positive location.

and manufactured to precise tolerances to accommodate 3,312 glass panels. We modified a robot that is commonly used in the automobile industry to cut the steel members in a computer-aided manufacturing process straight from the digital model. The members have a constant width, but the depth varies from member to member, and also 30 per cent of the members are tapered. During the cutting process the machine also marked the element number on to the upper side of each plate and marked centre, top and bottom of each node.

'The manufacturing sequence was the same as the installation sequence, and there was no lead time. Steel and glass were manufactured simultaneously. The steel members were then shipped to B&K Fabrications in Derby where they were assembled on jigs into a series of ladder trusses up to 10 metres in length. These were delivered to the site and lifted onto carefully placed props. The position of these props was critical for the precision of assembly. The next task for us was the assembly of the ladder trusses into lengths that could span from the reading room to the courtyard buildings.

'The deflection of the scaffold deck, due to the 500 tonnes of steel, needed to be factored in so that we could be confident of welding the sections together in the correct positions. During the process of the frame construction the position of each node needed to be monitored constantly to ensure precision. Every few days the props needed readjustment to counteract the increasing deflection of the scaffold deck.

The maximum tolerance between each structural node was only 3 millimetres. Once the 152 ladder trusses were installed the double-glassed panels, each of them a unique triangle, were placed. Now weighing 800 tonnes the entire roof was still resting on the props. Finally the props were carefully lowered until the roof came to rest on its bearings.

'During this process the roof was constantly being monitored to check its actual deformation against the anticipated one. The roof dropped 150 millimetres and spread 90 millimetres laterally as it settled. In other words, the structure was built in one shape, which was then "relaxed" into position. Since the exterior walls of the surrounding buildings could not receive any lateral forces the engineers at Buro Happold decided to rest the roof on sliding bearings, supported by a reinforced concrete beam that rests behind the parapets of the facades. The sliding bearings avoid the transferring of lateral forces into the facade, and so the weight is only transferred vertically. The reading room itself could not accept any lateral or vertical forces and so a series of load-bearing columns had to be constructed around its perimeter for the roof to rest on.'

Working with complex geometry constructions requires a careful calibration between the mutual influences of the boundary conditions and different parts of the as yet incomplete structural system during the assembly process. It is important to note that the successful incorporation of the many necessary adjustments to local structural components is a crucial development for the manufacturing and construction process of complex geometry structural systems. The planning of the assembly sequence requires the creative use of the stresses built up in

the unfinished structure during construction, and these will not be identical to the balanced forces in the final constructed piece.

'The 4,000-square-metre roof for the forum of the Sony Center in Berlin has a very complex elliptical geometry that spans 102 metres along the long axis and 77 metres along the shorter axis. The roof is made from 750 tonnes of steel, glass and a translucent fabric membrane. A steel framework ring-beam, which serves as the primary load-bearing part of the structure, sits on only seven bearings on top of the five buildings that make up the Sony Center. From this ring beam an inclined king post is suspended by means of steel cables. Due to the geometry and size of the ring beam it was impossible to transport preassembled parts of the beam to the site. The 11 geometrically different segments of the ring beam were constructed on site with the help of adjustable templates, lifted into place, welded together and subsequently lowered onto the bearings.

'The placement of the king post gave us the most difficult assembly problem. The king post was assembled from top to bottom in a supporting scaffold. The roof had to be built in a different shape to the final shape, which only appeared when the structure was complete and fully stressed. Our innovation was to design the inclined king post to work like an umbrella; shorter for the installation of the cables and membrane and then lengthened to stress the assembled structure. It took 1,500 tonnes of pressure to extend the king post. A crane with the 50-metre reach necessary for the assembly process was positioned on top of the inclined king post to optimise the effective working radius.

'After the completion and placement of the ring beam and the king post, the upper layer of 72 cables that carry the roof membrane and the lower layer of 16 cables that support the king post were assembled. Subsequently the king post was telescopically extended by 700 millimetres in order to prestress the cables. This prestressing took place over a period of several days to allow the fibres in the membrane to assume appropriate directionality. Further prestressing the tension elements of the structure compensated for the loss of tensioning in the membrane. Finally the glass elements were installed.'

The search for unusual solutions to complex geometrical problems necessitates the development of new methods and tools. Waagner Biro has developed its own digital tools and techniques for the integration of digital

'During this process the roof was constantly being monitored to check its actual deformation against the anticipated one. The roof dropped 150 millimetres and spread 90 millimetres laterally as it settled. In other words, the structure was built in one shape, which was then "relaxed" into position. Since the exterior walls of the surrounding buildings could not receive any lateral forces, the engineers at Buro Happold decided to rest the roof on sliding bearings, supported by a reinforced concrete beam that rests behind the parapets of the facades.'

'All software development is, of course, project driven, often requiring the programming of entirely new modules for each project, although some modules also carry over from project to project. Different projects pose different problems of rationalising geometry, of computational 3-D modelling that has to relate to either computer-aided manufacturing or fabrication instructions for complex manual manufacturing-and-assembly processes.'

modelling and computer-aided manufacturing. Customised software does not, however, provide the concept of fabrication and assembly, and this is where the engineering takes a creative step into new territory. In addition it is also necessary to develop calculation and testing procedures for these new types of structures.

'There are not many construction companies that can offer the combined knowledge, expertise and manufacturing capability in steel and glass that these kinds of projects require. It was necessary for us to create new methods and tools for modelling and construction, and the computer software we developed for these projects is now in constant use. We develop our own customised software and we have expertise in code writing. All software development is, of course, project driven, often requiring the programming of entirely new modules for each project, although some modules also carry over from project to project. Different projects pose different problems of rationalising geometry, of computational 3-D modelling that has to relate to either computer-aided manufacturing or fabrication instructions for complex manual manufacturing-and-assembly processes.

'The geometries we are now quite often dealing with pose difficult problems, particularly when the glass has to have flush outer surfaces and special frames for curved surfaces. The dome of the Reichstag, the facade of the Greater London Assembly and the Great Court roof were key projects for us in this respect. We soon realised that we were developing very special skills within our group for the manufacturing and

construction of complex geometry projects. Of course it was impossible to do this prior to recent computational development. However, computational expertise in modelling complex geometries for construction must be paralleled with manufacturing expertise. We collaborate very closely with our highly skilled workshop staff in the development of software and computer-aided manufacturing strategies and technologies.

'It is essential to establish the concept of fabrication and assembly very early in the design development. For computer-aided manufacturing the information has to be structured so that the relevant machine can directly read it. There is no manual interface, no hand in between to make adjustments by eye. The digital model or data set is continuous and flows straight to machine cutters. The manufacturing is fully integrated and all fabrication processes run from one and the same model.

'We confirm that the design works for the most extreme conditions, as the program must be run directly. Mock-ups of full-scale pieces and destructive load testing are sometimes required, but usually on typical connections, or on components instead of entire structures. We establish an intensive dialogue with the architects and engineers from the very beginning of the development, focusing on construction concepts and solutions with an emphasis on continual development. We have to make sure that we are never out of touch with the design concept and the necessary engineering knowledge, and we calculate all components, connections and assemblies many times over. Our collective experience yields a special kind of expertise that allows us to say that what looks odd is not necessarily wrong; it is just that we do not yet have an eye for such geometries.' ∆

Murphy/Jahn, Sony Center Forum Roof, Berlin, 2000
Opposite, top
The king post was telescopically extended by 700 millimetres over several days to prestress the structure, requiring 1,500 tonnes of pressure to do so.

Opposite, bottom, and above
The ring beam and the crane positioned on top of the inclined king post during assembly of the membrane and cables. The king post was designed to function like an umbrella, shorter for the installation of the cables and membrane and then lengthened to stress the assembled structure.

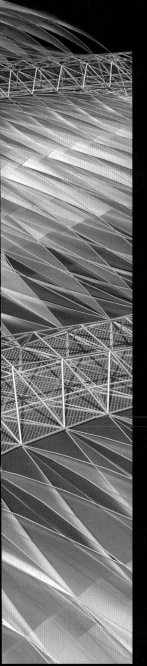

Approaching Complex Environments

The differentiation of material systems offers the possibility to develop an architectural approach that integrates ecological, topological and structural performances. Achim Menges presents two generative design strategies for differentiated structural systems approaching complex environments. They are explained alongside two of his projects – one derived from component proliferation and another derived from local manipulations of a larger global system.

Dense urban conglomerations have accelerated the effects of social, economic and environmental processes on the human environment. The increasing complexity of space-use cycles and material life cycles requires an understanding[1] of the built environment as ecological, topological and structural provisions that facilitate human activities.

Ecology refers to all the relationships between human groups and their physical and social environments. Topology is introduced here as the connections between all the material elements in an environment. Structure refers to organisational capacities above and beyond load bearing. In this way ecology, topology and structure are inseparably intertwined. These interrelations become instrumental when positive feedback between linked properties and their reciprocal influences modifies the generative process. The differentiation of a material system through a feedback process amplifies the dynamics of the environment. Emergent organisational effects then facilitate the mutation and migration of human activities.

The most important aspect of this approach is the emphasis on process and the acceleration of the evolution of an architectural environment, in which the relation of form and space to programme acknowledges the dynamic patterns of human habitation. Environment is understood as a dynamic composite of habitat-specific conditions and in habitant-specific itineraries, a gradient field of performative micro and macro milieus.[2] Together, these milieus produce an ecosystem, a dynamic relationship between environmental, topographical and structural intensities and human activities. Such an integral approach suggests that architectural design constitutes the modulation of micro-environmental conditions within an emergent macro-environmental system. It promotes modulations of the whole ecosystem, so that the architectural environment yields diverse and

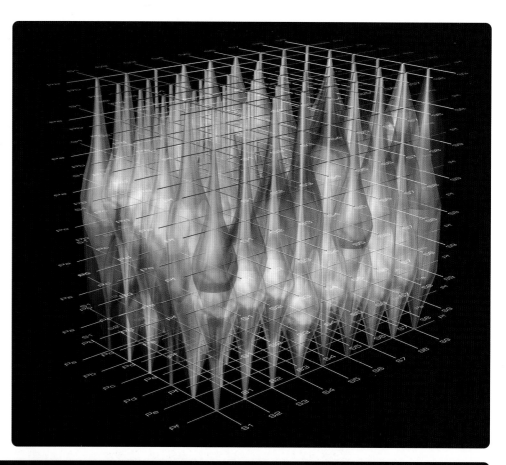

Postagriculture project

Opening spread
Proliferation of the surface component by parametric changes of the orientation, distribution, density and differential reinforcement of the seams, the depth and the internal pressure of the 'pneus', and the type and treatment of the surface material.

Above and right
Organisational model of differential intersystemic relations derived (above) by a digital-mapping technique of system-specific light and climatic conditions (right).

Below
Component evolution based on parametric variations of the boundary definition points, the seam layout, the pressure of the compressed air volume and the consequent geometry and prestressing of the membranes.

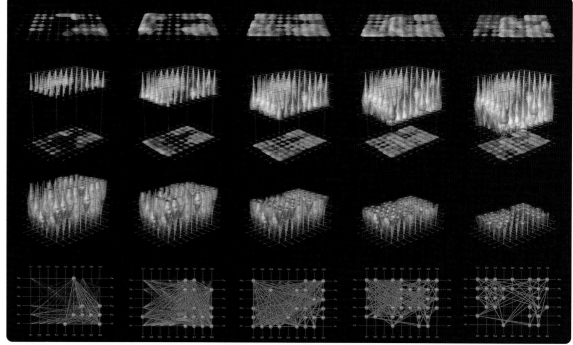

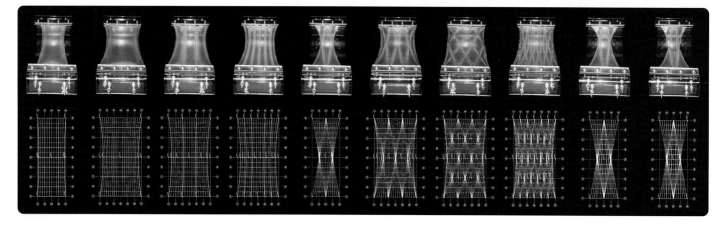

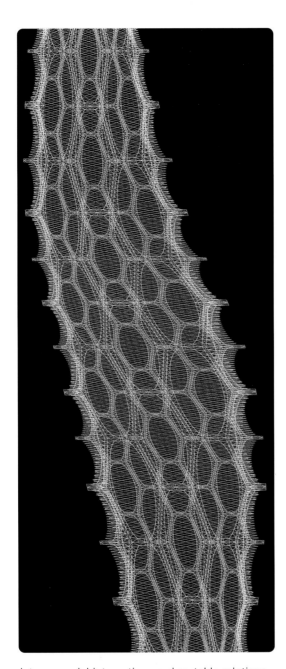

Above
Plan projection of the site-specific multilayered structural articulation of the Postagricultural landscape.

interrelations unfold in a nonlinear and complex manner, it is necessary to set up an operative design tool that recognises structural geometric behavioural patterns, corroborates qualitative difference and traces the inherent organisational logic of the system.

An account of two morpho-ecological design strategies is presented. These projects aim to generate complex environments that continue to evolve through adaptation, a process known as adaptiogenesis. Adaptation is based on evolutionary modifications and is the process of the continuous adjustment of a system to its environment. The two projects explore different ways of strategising morphological and ecological influences upon an evolutionary design process that aims to evolve a differentiated structural system. In Postagriculture, a research project for a large-scale agricultural production facility in the Netherlands, the design proceeded by strategic proliferation of a parametrically varied component into a larger differentiated system. The Landscape Playhouse, a competition design for the new Royal Theatre in Copenhagen, instrumentalises local manipulations within a global system.

The initial design criteria of the projects differ according to their contexts: the Playhouse in Copenhagen is located away from the main public street-life of the city centre. The intention is to create an urban environment that provides for a multitude of different activities and users, a piece of public fabric with its own rich urban life.

The Postagriculture project begins with the recognition of the importance of environmentally and socially sustainable food production. The project needed to negotiate multiple programmatic claims on a limited space. Its location in the Westland, the largest and densest greenhouse production area in the Netherlands, implies that this location needs to facilitate both time-intensive agricultural production (as outlined by the 5th Dutch National Planning Memorandum) and extensive public leisure activities (as requested by the municipal development plans of Rotterdam and the Hague) at the same time. The aim is to articulate an inclusive and responsive strategy, one that enables a mode of agricultural production that is a highly integrated, mutable and vital urban programme. The project promotes a local hybridisation of intensified agroproduction with public recreation. This in turn demands an architecture that is capable of negotiating and adapting to different system requirements.

Thus, the challenge of the Landscape Playhouse is the insufficient capacity of corridor and room arrangements to give access to public movement and activities, while the challenge of the Postagriculture project is to spatially combine activities that appear to be incompatible.

The approaches to both projects begin by establishing relevant performance criteria. In the case

intense social interactions and mutable relations between habitat and inhabitants. This is a shift from a unit-based design approach to condition-based design.

A condition-based approach involves generative feedback between digital and physical form finding, structural analysis and ecological testing techniques. The move away from 'morphographics' towards morphogenesis enables the projects to be developed from the bottom up. The evolution of material capacities and structural morphologies then leads to the emergence of an ecosystem. These morphogenetic processes are driven by the ability of matter to self-organise in relation to selected performance criteria. As morpho-ecological

Postagriculture project
Above
Perspective view of the deep
structure evolving from the
proliferation of parametrically
varied surface components.

of the Landscape Playhouse, mapping the required unit-based programmatic typologies on to a field of distributed condition-based activities made it possible to trace performance profiles. The organisational focus shifts to gradient topological and ecological conditions, such as the degree of connectivity or enclosure combined with the intensity of illumination, acoustics and climatic conditions.

For the Postagriculture project the systemic investigations were more complex. Parametric information about the climatic requirements of the agricultural and recreational systems and their subprocesses was used to build an organisational model. The model indicates specific condition profiles and differential relations, and system specificities emerge as

patterns of gradient thresholds and potentially shared conditions. The model is dynamic and is used for evolving the deployment of activities, organised by differential intensities of light, temperature and smell. It is employed to test internal developments and changes, and to absorb and reconfigure new information and external expertise, and establishes a continuous feedback loop enabling an intricate relation between analytical and generative modes.

Designing a performative, complex environment necessitates thinking about structure as a condition that generates and differentiates. It is helpful to think of structure not as a static object but rather as a process of material operations. Manipulations within the organisational logic and constraints of material systems are intrinsically connected to the modulation of microclimatic conditions.

Macro-environmental layout in
relation to recreational and
agricultural systems on the
project site.

Below
The performative environment
evolves from a tectonic
articulation that differentiates
through processes of material
operations (left). The deep
structure organises the
intersystemic connectivity
crucial to simultaneous, cyclic
processes of agricultural
production (middle) and
provides for gradient
transitions between hard-
modulated micro-environments
and negotiable fields of soft-
modulated areas (right).

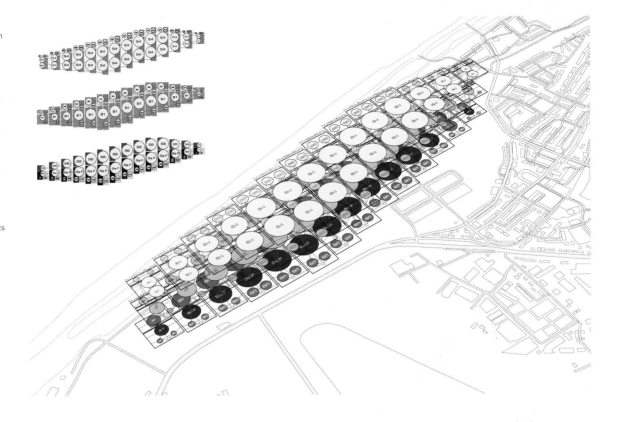

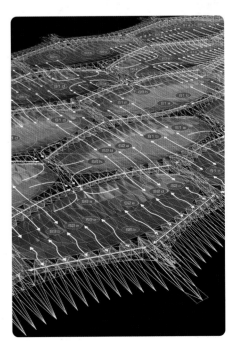

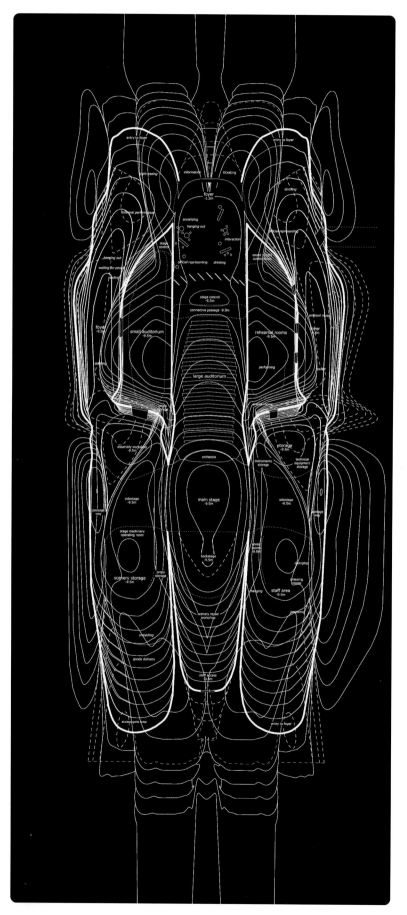

The differentiation process of the Postagriculture project is based on an investigation of one structural component, which indicates the possibilities and constraints of algorithmically controlled parametric variations in relation to selected performance criteria. Pneumatic structures were chosen for their potential for differentiation, which can be achieved by exploiting their nonlinear characteristics and differential states of stability. A pneumatic component – a specific pneu[3] – was evolved from a simple inflated cushion in which the basic structural principle is the relation between the pressure of the compressed air volume and the pre-stressing of the membranes. The working methodology was based on feedback between different modalities, using iterations of cycles between digital definitions of the boundary points, physical modelling derived from cutting-patterns produced in an engineering software program, empirical and digital form finding and digital structural analysis. By multiplying the evolved 'single cushion' component a prototype was developed – a multichambered surface component.

The relation of surface geometry to internal air pressure produces structural stability. This dynamic relation required the animation of boundary definition points that were then transferred back into the structural software package, providing the input for a digital form-finding process and enabling the production of a physical prototype. The resulting prototype has a number of forms and pressure states in which it is stable. This prototype is a self-supporting pneumatic surface, geometrically defined by different surface tensions and by seams that are structural elements. Parametric changes of variables such as the orientation, distribution, density and differential reinforcement of the seams, the depth and the internal pressure of the pneus, and the type and treatment of the surface material were all tested, analysed and catalogued in relation to their structural performance, topological characteristics and capacity to modulate light and climatic conditions.

An example of a morpho-ecological interrelation is the way the density of reinforced seams and their related structural capacity corresponds with the transmission of light and energy, influencing local illumination, temperature gradient and air movement. Another example is the nonlinear relation between the internal pressure and depth of the pneus, the related load-bearing capacity through prestressing the membrane, and the regulation of thermal conductivity through dead-air chambers. This data, and the related variations of assembled surfaces, feed the proliferation process of the component, producing a complex and differentiated system. The resulting 'deep' structure is a manifold of local geometries and ecosystems within a macro environment.

The feedback loop between material articulation and the modulation of interior conditions proceeds beyond

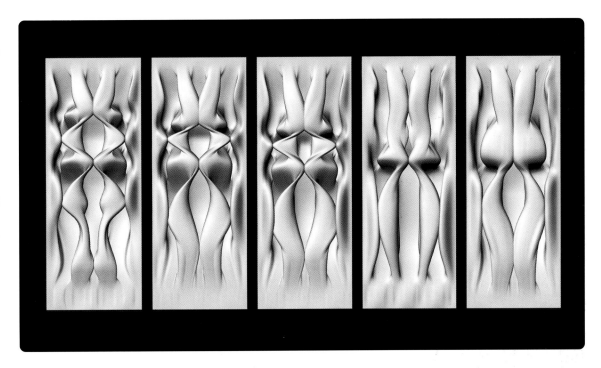

an understanding of structure as an accumulation of separate parts joined together. Structure here is a complex system, differentiated and performative. Digital simulations, with particular focus on temperature-scan and light analysis, show how the structure responds to locally specific load-bearing requirements, producing microclimatic differentiation. More importantly, the analysis of the structural and environmental performance also indicates the gradient transition from the hard-modulated micro-environments to a negotiable field of soft-modulated areas. These areas, which emerge in between the regulated material and surface manipulations, enable a robustness of distributed open systems over a broad range of conditions that can trigger and accommodate programmatic mutations.

The Landscape Playhouse project explores a different strategy. Here, the complexity of the global system emerges from distributed local manipulations within the structural field of a continuous surface. The correlation of local surface control points, principal surface curvature[4] and intersection, and geometrical, topological and structural logics is developed through an evolutionary process of digital and physical test-modelling and analysis. Initially the intersection of constant mean curvature surfaces[5] – surfaces with the same curvature at any point – indicated capacities for structural and topological differentiation. For example, the intersections of the surfaces become arch structures that redistribute forces so that the

material within the plane of the intersection becomes structurally redundant. These connective zones of the intersection carry the potential to modulate spatial as well as environmental conditions. Departing from constant curvature by developing the intersections as local moments of one larger self-intersecting surface suggested the possibility of gradually informing the interrelation between the intersection plane and local surface regions.

The geometric characteristics of these regions vary from synclastic to anticlastic articulation with related structural as well as topological capacities. Scripting them as local operations allowed the surface to adapt to site-specific trajectories and force fields, through an iterative sequence of test modelling and manipulation. The performative curvature and self-intersection of the surface has been informed by correlative digital and physical modelling, employing different CAD/CAM technologies. For example, monosectional and bidirectional laser-cut models inform sectional curvature studies, laser-sintered rapid prototypes investigate the differentiation of locally complex surface geometries negotiated by global tangency alignments, and 3-D-printed sectional models corroborate topological relations. These modalities and digital analysis techniques are combined within the process of surface evolution, and performance evaluation unfolds patterns of differentiated effects.

Further scripting, cataloguing and analysing geometric operations reveals the operative relation between locally manipulating the surface and modulating zones of different degrees of connectivity or enclosure and gradient intensities of climatic, noise and

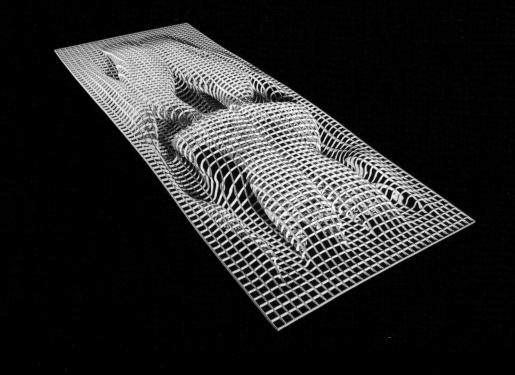

Landscape Playhouse project
Right
The performative curvature and self-intersection of the surface has been informed by correlative digital and physical modelling, employing different CAD/CAM technologies. For example, monosectional and bidirectional laser-cut models (top) inform sectional curvature studies, laser-sintered rapid prototypes (bottom) investigate the differentiation through locally complex surface geometries negotiated by the global tangency alignments, and 3-D-printed sectional models (middle) corroborated topological relations. Combining these modalities and digital-analysis techniques within the process of surface evolution and performance evaluation unfolds patterns of differentiated morpho-ecological effects.

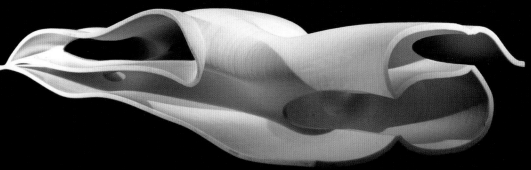

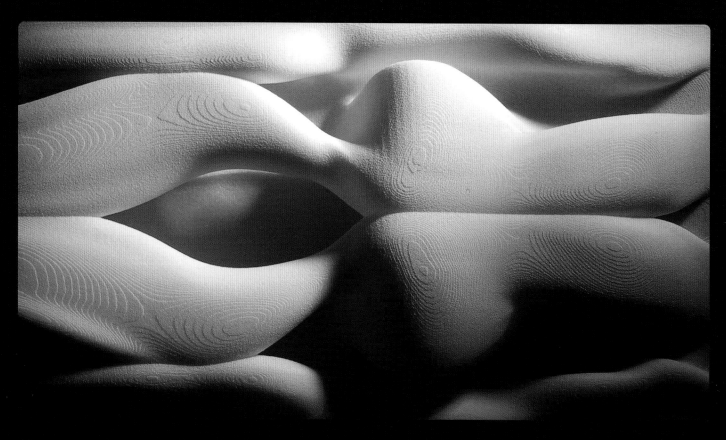

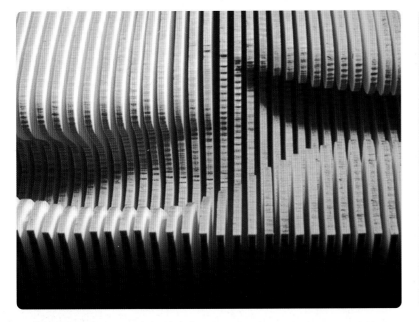

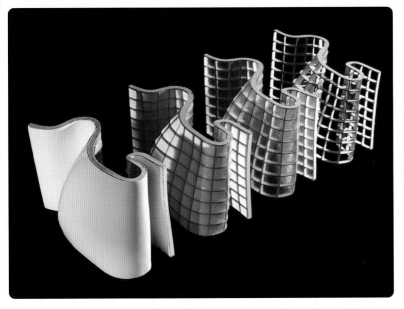

light conditions. The evolving structural characteristics of differential load distribution within this complex semi-monocoque shell also enabled a secondary system of differentiation. Necessary local surface penetrations are related to the varying load-bearing capacity of the surface. This means that, depending on the degree of stress within a particular local area of the shell, the surface area is punctuated by 'holes' filled with another material or sometimes no material. The new material has different transparencies and densities, leading to gradient fields of illumination and interiority that are intrinsically related to the structural performance of the system.

The dynamic interaction of multiple locally controlled surface definitions and penetrations

is an evolutionary process, one that evolves a complex global surface articulation that has interrelated structural, topological and ecological performances.

This approach is very different from more conventional deterministic strategies that match spatial units or locations with singular ways of inhabitation, the static neutrality of generic spaces that serve as a means of achieving 'flexibility'. In these projects both differentiation strategies[6] are part of design processes that relate the evolution of architectural form to environmental and social performance. The research suggests that alternative ideas of efficiency and sustainability of the built environment can be explored through adaptiogenesis. Structural 'efficiency' here evolves locally, by tracing and exploiting system characteristics that privilege material capacities. Consequently, larger material systems operate through implicitly adaptive redundancy. Through this process of bottom-up 'hyper-articulation', complex environments have the potential for inherent responsiveness, the ability to adapt to anticipated as well as divergent criteria.

The evolution of a differentiated genotypic organisation, based on the logic of the material system, leads to an intrinsically adaptive system of differentiated conditions and environments that enable activity migration and mutation. In addition, the evolutionary process enables a phenotypic plasticity[7] through active changes to structural spatial elements that locally adapt, triggering fields of potential inhabitation that are embedded in an ever-changing global organisation. In each case the architectural design is thought of as an ecosystem that organises the use of space in inclusive, time-based performance packages that allow for a denser and more differentiated environment. ⏃

Top left
Detail of monosectional laser-cut model.

Top right
Detail of laser-sintered rapid prototype surface.

Bottom
Skin evolution of semi-monocoque shell.

Since its inception, the Emergence and Design Group has collaborated with Professor George Jeronimidis at the Centre for Biomimetics of Reading University and Professor Birger Sevaldson at the Institute of Industrial Design at the Oslo School of Architecture. The focus of research is living nature's capacity to provide versatile models for design. Here, **Professor George Jeronimidis** examines natural dynamic systems, material behaviour and adaptation, and presents the case for implementation of these models in architecture and engineering.

The developments in smart materials and responsive buildings are at the forefront of scientific and technical advances in engineering and have stimulated a renewed interest in biology and biomimetics.[1] Whilst there have been a number of interesting architectural applications of advanced materials in architecture, we cannot say that intelligent buildings exist. Environmentally responsive systems for buildings have certainly made rapid advances in the last decade, but they function as a collection of devices such as louvres and shades, controlled by a central computer that receives data from remote sensors and sends back instructions for activation of mechanical systems.

This is essentially a 19th-century concept, even if human decision-making has been replaced by computational decision-making. Natural systems are quite different. Most sensing, decision-making and reactions are entirely local, and global behaviour is the product of local actions. This is true across all scales, from small plants to large mammals. When we run for the bus, we do not have to make any conscious decisions to accelerate our heartbeat, increase breathing rate and volume, or to open our pores to regulate the higher internal temperatures generated. Plants, lacking a central nervous system and mammalian brains, make growth movements to orientate themselves to the sun or to correct their inclination.

In order to abstract engineering principles for use in architecture, we must first recognise that we are studying material systems in which it makes little sense to distinguish between material and structure. Further, we must recognise that all

natural material systems involve movement – both local and global – to achieve adaptation and responsiveness. There has been little systematic engineering study of dynamic systems in nature, and in particular of the way in which many biological material systems achieve movement without muscles.

Geometry and Fibre Material Hierarchies

In the morphogenesis of biological organisms, it is the animation of geometry and material that produce form. Dynamic capacity, the ability to move, is created by the same factors. Geometry and material hierarchies produce dynamics. Biodynamics are achieved by a system of pre-tensioning and variation of turgor pressure[2] in differentiated geometrical arrangements to produce different kinds of movements. Many animals with flexible skins, such as worms and sharks, use hydrostatic skeletons where the prestressing of fibres in tension is balanced by compression in a fluid. Similarly, nonlignified plants are entirely dependent on control of turgor pressure inside their cells to achieve structural rigidity, prestressing the cellulose fibres in the cell walls at the expense of compression in the fluid. Trees prestress their trunks, too, with the outermost layers of cells being prestressed in tension to offset the poor compressive properties of wood.[3]

Biology makes use of remarkably few materials, and nearly all loads are carried by fibrous composites. There are only four polymer fibres: cellulose in plants, collagen in animals, chitin in insects and crustaceans, and silks in spiders' webs. These are the basic materials of biology, and they have much lower densities than most engineering materials. They are successful not so much because of what they are but because of the way in which they are put together. The geometrical and hierarchical organisation of the fibre architecture is significant. The same collagen fibres are used in low-modulus, highly extensible structures such as blood vessels, intermediate-modulus tissues such as tendons and high-modulus rigid materials such as bone.

Fibre composites are anisotropic, a characteristic that can provide higher levels of optimisation than is possible with isotropic, homogeneous materials, because stiffness and strength can be matched to the direction and magnitude of the loads applied. It is growth under stress; the forces that the organism experiences during growth produce selective deposition of new material where it is needed and in the direction in which it is needed. In bone, material is removed from the under-stressed parts and redeposited in the highly stressed ones;[4] in trees a special type of wood, with a different fibre orientation and cellular structure from normal wood, is produced in successive annual rings when circumstances require it.[5] Thus biology produces a large number of patterns of load-bearing fibre architectures,

Opening spread
The bony lamellae of the femur, made of compacted collagen fibres and minerals. During self-formation a matrix is laid down in lamellar, sheet-like form which is mineralised by calcium phosphate crystals.

Opposite
Section through the stem of a buttercup showing the oval vascular bundle at the centre that contains xylem vessels and supporting tissue.

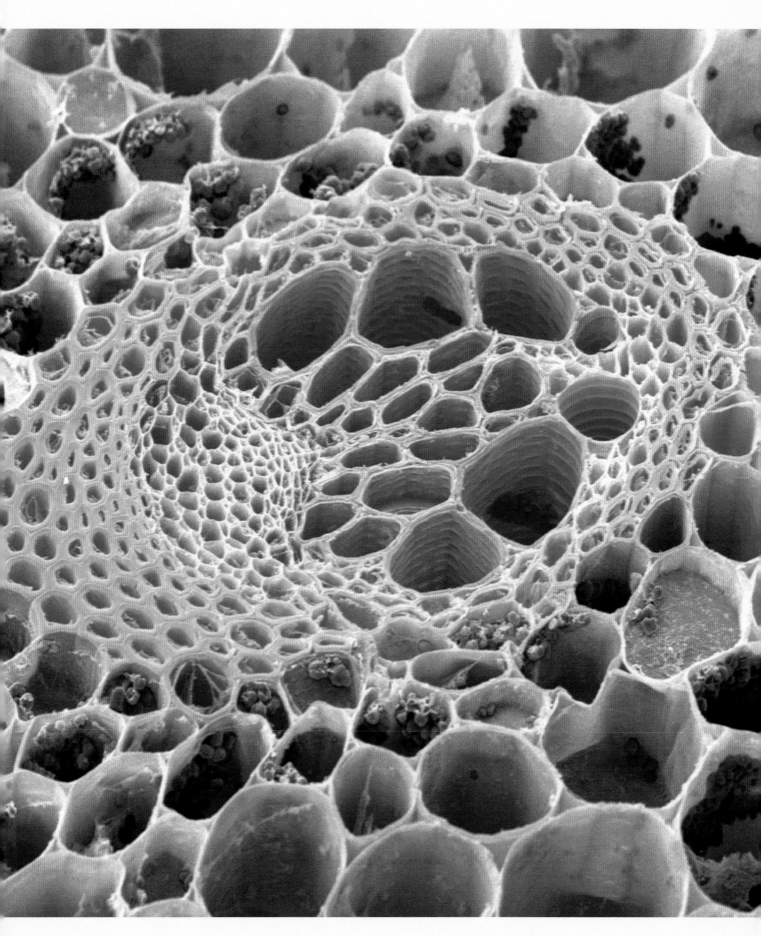

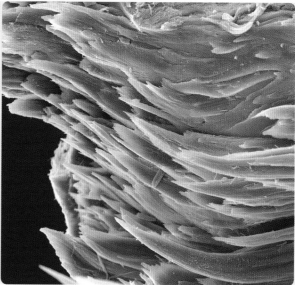

each a specific answer to a specific set of mechanical conditions and requirements.[6]

Fibres are most efficient when they carry pure tensile loads, either as structures in their own right or as reinforcement in composite materials that are used as membrane structures in biaxial tension.[7] Fibres perform poorly in compression because of buckling, even when partially supported laterally by the matrix in composites. In nature there are a number of available solutions to this problem: prestress the fibres in tension so that they hardly ever experience compressive loads; introduce high-modulus mineral phases intimately connected to the fibres to help carry compression; or heavily cross-link the fibre network to increase lateral stability, and change the fibre orientation so that compressive loads do not act along the fibres.

Movement Without Muscles

Many plants are capable of movement. Slow movements often pass unremarked, even though they are very familiar, such as those seen in the petals of flowers that open and close, the tracking of the sun by sunflowers, the convolutions of bindweeds around supporting stems and the snaking of roots around obstacles. Rapid movements are more visible, such as the closing and drooping of leaves when *Mimosa pudica* is touched. Very rapid movements, too fast to be seen, are exceptional, but do occur in the closing of the leaves of the Venus flytrap. And the most common of all movements is the shedding of leaves in the autumn, which is not a passive mechanism but an active one. In all these examples, movement and force are generated

by a unique interaction of materials, structures, energy sources and sensors.

Movements that are reversible in plants are produced by pressure changes within special cells. These parenchyma cells are flexible in bending but stiff in tension; when a cell takes in water, the pressure exerted on its walls increases, and the cell increases in size due to the elasticity of its walls. If the pressure of neighbouring cells increases at the same time, the tensions result in deformations of the whole tissue, which causes movement of part of the plant. The arrangement of cells of different sizes and orientations constrains the movement in the direction that is needed. When the osmotic pressure[8] within the cells slowly decreases, the movement is reversed. A common example of this mechanism is the daily lifting and lowering of leaves in a day/night cycle.

These material systems are essentially working as networks of interacting mini-hydraulic actuators, liquid-filled bags which can become turgid or flaccid and which, owing to their shape and mutual interaction, translate local deformations to global ones and are capable of generating very high stresses.

The same mechanism is used within the tissue of the leaf, where the stomata regulate the respiration of the plant. Stomata open when the air is humid, and close when it is dry. The mechanism is differential pressure in an asymmetrical arrangement of cells. The outer and inner walls are much thicker than the lateral walls, and so have greater resistance to deformations. The thinner areas are more easily stretched. The asymmetry of the cell's structure and of the wall thicknesses directs the movement caused by the pressure changes. There are two controlling cycles, of water and of carbon dioxide, which at times may compete, as carbon dioxide can limit photosynthesis. Light stimulates the stomata to open, and they close at night except in very arid

Above left
Ripe seed capsule of the field poppy, showing the release of seeds by the self-organised process of dehiscence (dehydration and splitting).

Above right
A freeze-fractured tendon revealing the parallel structure of collagen fibres of varying size. The parallel organisation produces a structure that is flexible but inelastic and able to resist tension.

Opposite
Human collagen-fibre bundles made up of three long polypeptide chains that self-assemble into triple-helix fibrils, extensively cross-bonded to form a strong inextensible structure.

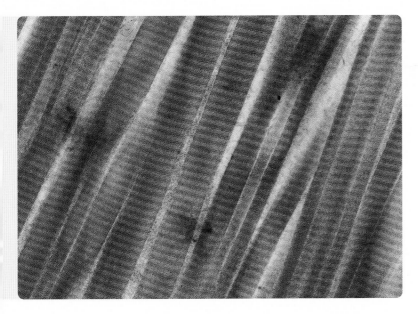

Notes
1 GR Tomlinson and WA Bulloch, 'Smart Materials and Structures', *Proceedings of the 4th European and 2nd MIMR Conference*, Harrogate, July 1998 (Institute of Physics, Bristol).
2 When plant cells take in water by osmosis they start to swell, but the cell wall prevents them from bursting. Plant cells become 'turgid', which means swollen and hard. Turgor pressure is liquid or hydrostatic pressure, and turgidity is what makes the green parts of the plant 'stand up'.
3 RR Archer, *Growth Stresses and Strains in Trees*, Springer Verlag (Berlin), 1986.
4 JD Currey, *The Mechanical Adaptation of Bone*, Princeton University Press (Princeton, NJ), 1984.
5 Archer, op cit.
6 AC Neville, *Biology of Fibrous Composites*, Cambridge University Press (Cambridge), 1986.
7 M Elices (ed), *Structural Biomaterials*, Princeton University Press (Princeton, NJ), 2000.
8 The pressure created when water flows by osmosis through a semipermeable membrane into a chamber containing a high concentration of solutes.
9 H Kobayashi, B Kresling and JFV Vincent, 'The geometry of unfolding tree leaves', *Proceedings of the Royal Society of London*, 1998, pp 147–54.
10 JA Trotter and TJ Koob, 'Collagen and proteoglycan in a sea urchin ligament with mutable mechanical properties, *Cellular Tissue*, 1989, pp 258, 527.

climates where the cycle is reversed to prevent water losses.

If the pressure change cannot be reversed, the pressure builds beyond the ability of the tissue to resist the force. The tissue will rupture in the weakest area. Weak areas are carefully placed, so that the orientation and speed of the rupture is controlled. This mechanism is designed for the explosive movements or catapult actions of some fruits.

The fruits of all *Impatiens* plants have specially formed weaker tissues along which the ruptures will propagate, severing the longitudinal connections between the carpels, which instantly roll up and catapult the seeds away. The squirting cucumber, *Ecballium elaterium*, uses the same mechanism to discharge its seeds at such high velocity that a distance of up to 10 metres is achieved. Similar mechanisms can be seen in operation when leaves emerge from buds and deploy to catch sunlight. The packing of the maximum surface area of material in the bud and expanding it rapidly and efficiently is the result of very clever folding geometry, turgor pressure and growth.[9]

Variable-Stiffness Material Systems

Evolutionary adaptive mechanical design in natural material systems occurs at the level of the species, in response to a set of inputs on the developing organism. The inputs include loads and environmental pressures that interact with the genetic information available. Evolutionary time is very long, but evolutionary adaptation can be successfully modelled in computational processes and is useful in design strategies for the development of architecture in series, types

and populations. There are two other aspects of biological adaptation that occur over much shorter time scales, which involve individuals rather than whole species and are thus more observable.

Thigmomorphogenesis is the changes in shape, structure and material properties that are produced in reponse to transient changes in environmental conditions. Tropisms of various kinds are also observable, such as heliotropism in sunflowers. These are all growth movements, slow adaptations to changes in specific conditions. The formation of reaction wood in trees, needed to straighten a trunk towards the vertical when it has experienced inclined growth or to offset loads from prevailing winds, and the mechanism of bone remodelling are perhaps the best known and best documented examples. Fibre orientations, structural capacities and properties of materials are modified by slow movements within a material; these are not yet available in industrial materials, but it is clear that this should be the goal of longer-term research.

There are many instances in engineering where variable-stiffness materials and structures would be beneficial. For example, this is particularly true for vibration control, and in applications where it would be beneficial to alter the shape of a rigid structure, or an element of structure, and then restiffen it. Potential architectural applications are structures that could be reconformed for change of load or condition, and portable structures that could be soft for transportation, rigid in deployment and soft again for relocation.

There are several examples of this in biology that offer interesting models that are more immediately achievable. The most interesting is the variable-stiffness collagen found in many marine animals.[10] It is found in sea cucumbers and also at the base of spines in sea urchins. In this system, the collagen fibres are embedded in a matrix that can be changed from rigid to nearly liquid. In the liquid, low-stiffness state the collagen fibres act as uncoupled elements and do not have any reinforcing effect. When the matrix is hardened by the release of calcium ions, the efficiency of load transfer between matrix and fibres increases and the composite becomes rigid. The sea cucumber goes soft when threatened and flows away; the sea urchin softens the anchorage of its spines when it wants to move and can relock the system in a new location.

The study of biodynamics offers models for dynamic material systems and for adaptation. Scale has to be carefully considered if principles are abstracted from biodynamic systems for use in architecture. Forces increase exponentially when differential pressure systems are enlarged. The geometrical organisation and fibre patterns are scaleable, and with 'muscle-less' movement and stiffness variability suggest a means of achieving significantly advanced architectural material systems. ∆

Martin Hemberg is a PhD student at the Department of Bioengineering at Imperial College, London. His area of research is complex systems and he is particularly interested in emergence, self-organisation and morphogenesis. He holds an MSc in engineering physics from Chalmers University of Technology, and a BSc in economics from the University of Gothenburg. In 2001 he joined the Emergent Design Group at MIT and participated in the development of Genr8 as his master's thesis. After moving to London in 2003 he began teaching at the Emergent Technologies and Design masters programme at the Architectural Association.

Michael Hensel is an architect and partner in OCEAN NORTH and the Emergence and Design Group. He is director of the Emergent Technologies and Design masters programme and unit master of Diploma Unit 4 at the Architectural Association School of Architecture. He has taught, lectured and published in Europe, the Americas and the Middle and Far East.
www.ocean-north.org
www.emergence-and-design.org www.aaschool.ac.uk/et

George Jeronimidis is professor of composite materials engineering at the University of Reading and director of the Centre for Biomimetics. He studied physical chemistry at the University of Rome and worked as research scientific officer for a few years after his PhD before moving to Britain in 1971. His teaching and research interests are in design with composite materials, mechanical design of biological systems and biomimetics. He has lectured on these subjects in several courses in the UK and abroad and, for the past three years, has taught a course on biomimetics as part of the Emergent Technologies and Design masters programme at the Architectural Association School of Architecture.

Wolf Mangelsdorf studied architecture and civil engineering at Karlsruhe University, where he also worked for an architectural practice after graduation. After research at Kyoto University he moved to Britain in 1997 and became a design engineer for Anthony Hunt Associates, working in the firm's Cirencester and London offices. Since 2002 he has been an associate with Buro Happold in London and is currently project leader for a number of projects including the refurbishment of Battersea Power Station. For the past three years he has taught advanced structures at the Architectural Association, and is a faculty member of Emergent Technologies and Design.

Achim Menges is an architect and partner in OCEAN NORTH and the Emergence and Design Group. He studied at the Technical University of Darmstadt and graduated from the Architectural Association School of Architecture with honours. He currently teaches Diploma Unit 4 and the Emergent Technologies and Design masters programme at the AA School. He received the Far Eastern International Digital Architectural Design (FEIDAD) Outstanding Design Award in 2002 and the FEIDAD Design Merit Award in 2003.
www.achimmenges.net
www.emergence-and-design.org
www.ocean-north.net
www.aaschool.ac.uk/et

Farshid Moussavi studied at University College London, the Bartlett School of Architecture and Dundee University, and received a masters degree from Harvard Graduate School of Design in 1991. Prior to establishing Foreign Office Architects (with Alejandro Zaera Polo) she worked with the Renzo Piano Building Workshop in Genoa and the Office for Metropolitan Architecture in Rotterdam in 1992. She is currently professor of architecture at the Academy of Fine Arts in Vienna, has previously taught at the Architectural Association School of Architecture (1993–2000) and has been visiting professor at the University of California in Los Angeles, Columbia University in New York, Princeton University, the Berlage Institute in Amsterdam and the Hoger Architecture Institute in Belgium.

Una-May O'Reilly is a research scientist. She is a fellow of the Artificial Intelligence Laboratory at MIT, where she specialises in humanoid robotics-based artificial intelligence, and a fellow of the Santa Fe Institute for the Study of Complex Systems. Her extensive research includes evolutionary algorithms and the theory and analysis of genetic programming. She has won numerous honours and awards and has published widely on these topics.

Charles Walker heads the Advanced Geometry Unit at Arup & Partners. He is both a chartered architect and engineer, and has worked with many renowned architects including Toyo Ito, OMA, UN Studio, Daniel Libeskind and, more recently, Oscar Niemeyer. He was recently a member of the winning design team for the Grand Egyptian Museum, with Henegan Peng Architects. Among other structures, he was responsible for the domes at the Singapore Arts Centre (while a director at Atelier One).

Michael Weinstock is an architect, and is co-director of the Emergent Technologies and Design masters programme, master of technical studies at the Architectural Association School of Architecture, and a founder member of the Emergence and Design Group. His research interests lie in exploring the convergence of biomimetic engineering, emergence and material sciences, and he has taught and published on these topics since 1994.
www.aaschool.ac.uk/et

Chris Wise is director of expedition engineering and professor of creative design at Imperial College, London. He joined Ove Arup & Partners in 1979, became director in 1992, and was later appointed one of five board directors. He was awarded the distinction of Royal Designer for Industry by the Royal Society of Arts, and in 2002 received an honorary fellowship of the Royal Institute of British Architects. He lectures, writes and broadcasts widely, in the UK, Europe and the US, on creative design in projects and the role of the engineer in design.

Alejandro Zaera Polo studied at the ETS of Architecture in Madrid and received a masters degree from Harvard Graduate school of Design in 1991. With Farshid Moussavi, he founded Foreign Office Architects in 1992. Besides his architectural work, he has been a visiting critic in the US at Princeton University, the University of California in Los Angeles and Columbia University; and in Europe at the Berlage Institute in Amsterdam, where he is currently dean. His critical and theoretical work has been published in international magazines.

98+   Interior Eye   Retail in the Dumpster
Craig Kellogg

101+   Building Profile   The Kunsthaus at Graz
Jeremy Melvin

106+   Practice Profile   Dale Jones-Evans
Leon van Schaik

114+   Engineering Exegesis   Blurring the Lines:
The Chesa Futura
André Chaszar

118+   From Political Reportage to *Prêt-à-Porter*
Eleanor Curtis

120+   Book Reviews

122+   Supercrit #1 and #2
Samantha Hardingham

125+   Book Club

126+   Site Lines   A Sort of Homecoming:
The Art Gallery of Ontario
Sean Stanwick

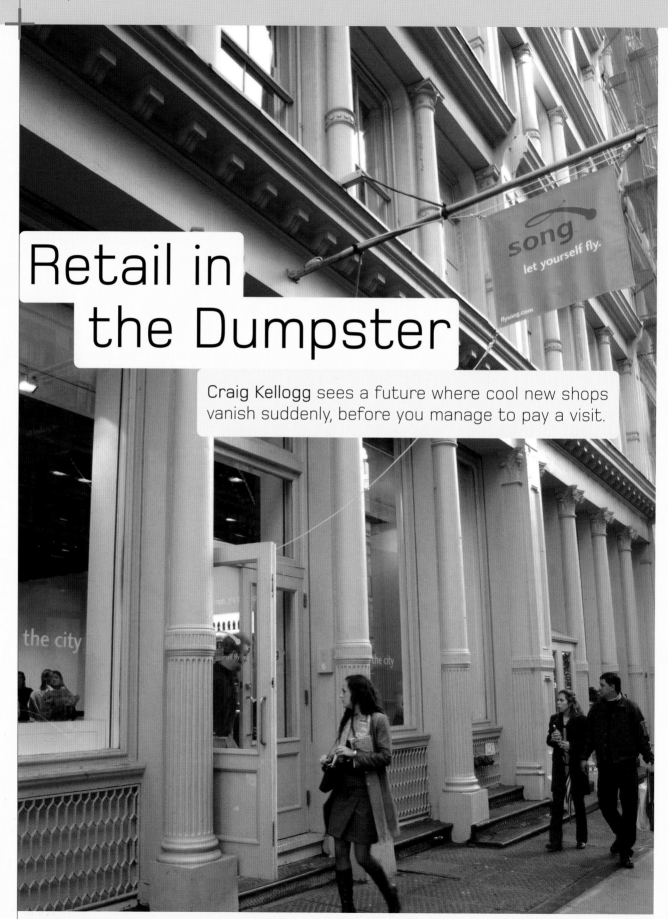

Below
A restored cast-iron shop front on New York's Prince Street was the temporary home of Song in the City, a retail space operated briefly by Song, a fledgling US airline. Song chose SoHo for its ability to attract passers-by in a target demographic: stylish young women who shop.

Retail in the Dumpster

Craig Kellogg sees a future where cool new shops vanish suddenly, before you manage to pay a visit.

Below left
The development team found a nearly finished shop front for the
venture, which featured discrete activity zones within an open plan.

Below right
Souvenir merchandise was collected within reusable showcases
that the airline expects to recycle for shops in subsequent cities.

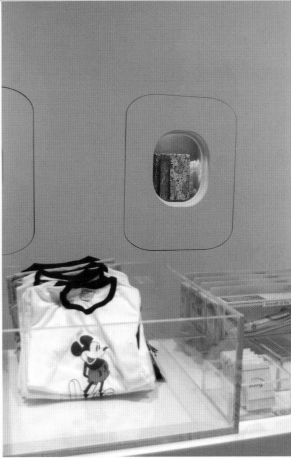

Always a gamble, retail looks particularly risky during an
economic slump. Then, in a domino effect, blight may descend
on gap-toothed urban shopping streets. But every failure is
an opportunity, too. To fill reasonably priced vacant shops in
Manhattan, a new concept is emerging, one that is ideal for
uncertain economic times. Call it stunt retail. 'Disposable'
shops can fill vacancies for just a month or two, as they feed
off the media frenzy that accompanies the launch of a hot
new boutique. Then, just when the thrill begins to recede,
disposable shops can quietly disappear.

Manhattan has long had temporary bazaars offering small
selections of seasonal merchandise. As recently as last autumn,
Bluefly, the internet fashion retailer, opened a 'loft-like' shop
in Manhattan to clear merchandise that remained in quantities
too limited to sell online. But such seasonal shopkeepers tend
not to invest much time and creativity in design beyond the
necessary tables for cashiers and blazing fluorescents overhead.
The new breed of disposable shops, however, are anything
but bare-bones boxes, as the financial backing for these
enterprises often comes from major corporations.

For the launch of a new line of discount fashions by the
flamboyant American designer Isaac Mizrahi, Target, a
suburban big-box retailer, opened a bustling boutique in
Manhattan's Rockefeller Center. Avi Adler Inc, a Modernist
florist and events planner, supervised the job. Innovative
materials created the feeling of a cheerful advertising

campaign. Instead of regular wallpaper, design partner
David Stark used Tyvek, a pearly nonwoven fabric
typically buried in the wood-framed walls of residential
construction as a moisture barrier. Inexpensive particle
board was milled into display niches. 'It's not what you
use,' Stark told the New York Times, 'it's how you use it.'
Disposable elements like the dressing rooms – simple
felt-curtained cylinders – were easy to dismantle when
the shop was shut down. You can imagine the whole
affair as it must have ended up when the party ended –
speeding down the New Jersey Turnpike squashed into
the corner of a rusty dumpster.

Song Airlines, a new bargain carrier affiliated with
the US behemoth Delta Air Lines, opened its own
disposable shop and gallery last autumn in a historic
cast-iron building in Manhattan's SoHo. The first
important decision concerned the location itself.
Finished spaces that could be easily transformed
seemed to offer the advantage of both speed and
economy. Song also wanted high-speed internet
connections and plenty of basement storage space.
The company's creative team settled on an empty Prince
Street shop front nicely finished by its previous tenant,
the Shiseido cosmetics company. Not coincidentally,
Song's target demographic is precisely the same
customer. Market research had indicated that the vast

Below left
The lounge area's false ceiling approximated the look of an aircraft cabin.

Below right
Video monitors installed near the front window by the previous tenant
were readily adapted for their new purpose with Song programming.

majority of online travel purchases are made by free-spending, stylish young women who carry designer purses and control the family purse strings.

From the contents to the colour scheme, Song's shop and gallery therefore exhibited a canny gender bias. Where most American airlines are red, white and blue, the Song interiors palette displayed the company's signature rainbow of 14 sunny shades, from grapefruit to dark tangerine, blueberry and creamy avocado. Relatively inexpensive supergraphics also helped to transform the walls, with a giant blue map indicating Song's routes and destinations: 15 airports in 13 cities, and counting.

Consistent with the business model of a discount carrier, the budget for building and running the space was less than US$2 million. Adequate elements such as the existing ceiling were simply painted. Monitors in mirrored frames left behind by Shiseido were reprogrammed to show Song videos to passers-by. Anyone lured through the front doors by the videos found a series of discrete activity zones within an open plan. A café flanked the entrance, and at the centre of the space visitors tested actual aircraft seats as they sat in front of the same satellite broadcasts enjoyed by Song passengers. There

was also a retail display of souvenir merchandise in showcases modelled on aircraft windows. Some things were from Manhattan accessories designer Kate Spade, who also designed the airline's uniforms.

Mixing metaphors, the 'departure lounge' had portholes backed with video screens looped to simulate flight. (The airline hired an artist to fly in one of its planes and videotape the clouds and sunset while descending into Las Vegas.) Overhead, in the lounge, a surprisingly elaborate new arched false ceiling evoked the shape of an aircraft cabin. Obviously expensive, the arched ceiling would seem an elaborate gesture at odds with the ephemeral nature of the shop. But Song will recycle such durable modular elements as temporary shops open in subsequent cities. Even before the Manhattan shop closed, the search was on for a suitable space in Boston. Working in reverse, new architectural elements and the familiar modular ones will transform totally raw space. 'We are extremely happy with the New York project,' said Stacy Geagan, Song's director of public relations. 'And we would be looking to create a perfect replica.' Ɑ

Building Profile

Below
View from the Schlössberg. In form and material the Kunsthaus may be an alien presence, but it also seems an appropriate and welcome one.

The Kunsthaus at Graz

For the Austrian city of Graz, Peter Cook and Colin Fournier have created a contemporary art centre with an 'amorphic, perimeter-hugging form' that has already been dubbed by locals 'the friendly alien'. Jeremy Melvin explains how the drama of the Kunsthaus befits not only its 19th-century context but also its task as a gallery space that incites interaction.

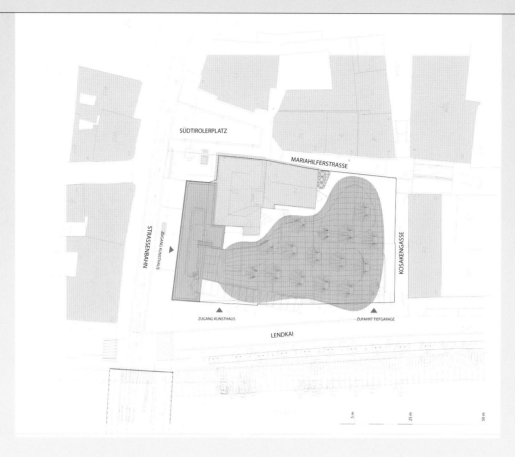

Like most of Austria, Graz – Europe's cultural capital for 2003 – is polite and wears its uniforms well. The principal difference is that here the uniforms are not just splendid scenery and gorgeous relics of an imperial past, though it certainly does have a wonderful natural setting, ringed by peaks with the River Mur running through a gorge deep enough to prevent melting snow flooding the city, and its very own captive mountain, the Schlössberg, which as its name suggests was forced into subservience when a castle was built on its summit. Its sunlight, casting intricate detail on the traditional buildings into sharp relief, is such that you realise you are within spitting distance of Italy, but a glimpse of the Hotel Weisler, designed by a pupil of Otto Wagner, recalls the proximity of Vienna. Sit in a café here, Peter Cook explains, and you will feel your neighbours stiffen respectfully when a canon of the cathedral walks past.

Graz's other uniform also manifests itself socially, architecturally and intellectually. Scientists at the university have won numerous Nobel prizes over the last couple of decades, as Cook's co-designer, Colin Fournier, is quick to point out. And there is a strong literary tradition, which arose in part because Graz took the lead in establishing a post-Nazi Austrian culture. In architecture the Grazer Schule has pioneered a language of contemporary materials, the striking forms of which speak as much of context as of deconstruction, and it is from this nexus of tradition and innovation that Cook's and Fournier's Kunsthaus takes its place in the urban and social fabric.

Shaped as if it has landed on its site, the Kunsthaus's bulbous blue form provoked the soubriquet 'the friendly alien' –

appropriately, perhaps, because it is on the side of the river that saw the typical paraphernalia of 19th-century urban expansion that could not be accommodated in the traditional city centre. A century ago, grand hotels and railway stations were probably just as alien, and Eiserners Haus, the iron-framed former department store that the Kunsthaus incorporates, was made entirely from components manufactured in south Yorkshire.

Graz has numerous museums, ranging from Renaissance *palazzi* to white boxes, but the whole ethos of a post-Bilbao contemporary arts centre depends on an arresting and unexpected image in a part of town that needs regeneration. It was perhaps this underlying truth that scuppered an earlier proposal that the Kunsthaus be formed from converting wartime air-raid shelter tunnels in the Schlössberg, which lies on the posher side of the river. Cook and Fournier were unplaced in that competition, but made enough powerful friends to be in a strong position when the scheme foundered and the new site was chosen. Their earlier entry also had the inestimable value of familiarising them with the specific functional requirements, from the secure delivery facilities to the ancillary and administrative activities, as well as the gallery spaces themselves.

The Kunsthaus is obviously within the tradition of contemporary arts centres that have covered Europe from Helsinki to Santiago di Compostella, and like them has specific economic parameters. The site is

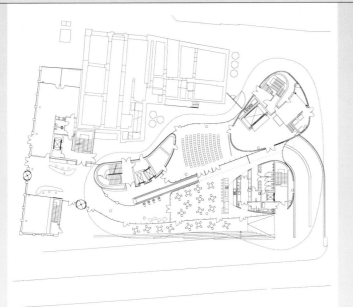

The organic form of the Kunsthaus fits within the site parameters, incorporating the Eiserners Haus, and abutting a pair of nondescript 18th-century town houses that are due to become an architecture centre.

Opposite
Site plan.

Top
Ground (entrance level), showing the entrance through the Eiserners Haus and location of the café and lecture room.

Middle left
The lower of the principal gallery levels. Within the irregularities of wall and travolators, there is plenty of space for flexible layouts.

Middle right
Diagram showing structural concept and position of cowls.

Bottom left
The upper of the exhibition galleries, showing the position of the cowls and the needle.

Bottom right
Long section. The galleries are contained within their own form, which is reached by travolator.

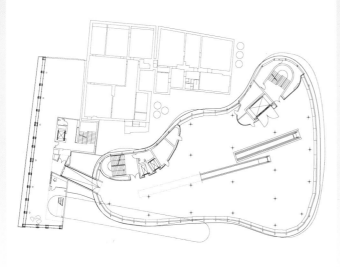

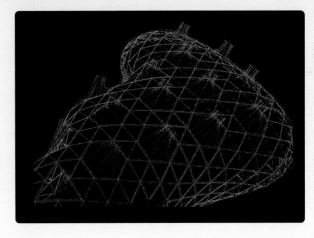

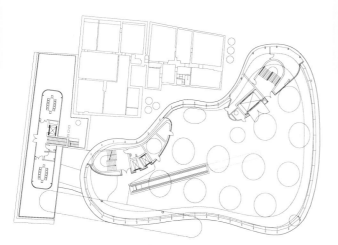

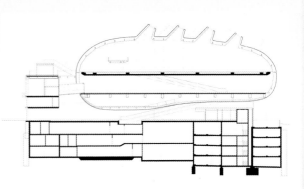

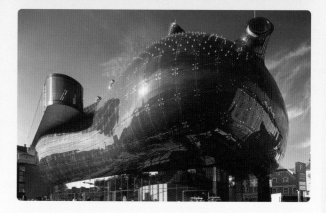

not overly generous and any project with the required accommodation would be likely to cover its entire surface area, and need more than one storey. There was also the Eiserners Haus to incorporate, which, as it turned out, needed almost complete rebuilding. These conditions did not inevitably lead to Cook's and Fournier's design as the only logical solution, but they do make sense of its amorphic, perimeter-hugging form, and of the essential drama with which it is infused, especially in the pair of travolators that switch back on each other as they take visitors from ground to first, and then to the upper level. With the entrance at ground level through the austere, almost peristyle Eiserners Haus, with offices on its upper levels, and ancillary functions such as a café and lecture room on the ground floor of the Kunsthaus proper, the two main exhibition spaces, on two levels, could take uninhibited possession of the flowing form.

These levels are generously serviced to facilitate a wide range of installations and their size minimises the effect of the serpentine perimeter, should anyone want an orthogonal layout. Modulated daylight can come into the top floor though the roof-top cowls, which from the exterior resemble bubbles bursting in the viscous droplet. Perched precariously across the top, again suggesting an analogy with the surface tension of liquids, is the 'needle', an observation platform that the engineer, Klaus Bollinger, allowed to vibrate slightly. Overall the effect is one of invisibly arrested flow, as if the building itself is a brief episode of calm in the flux of contemporary art, which makes a neat metaphor for the way an exhibition will always be historical even when its subject matter is of living artists. With an easily locatable entrance and logical disposition of basic functions, it is easy to appreciate the building at an immediate level, but its facade is deliberately inscrutable to conceal the specifics of any exhibition.

Opposite, top left
Roof view of one of the
Kunsthaus cowls. These might
be safety valves releasing
pressure from inside.

Opposite, top right
Night view.

Opposite, bottom left
Historical view of the
Eiserners Haus. Austrians
have always been keen on
uniforms and uniformity.

Opposite, bottom right
The conjunction of forms
intrigues as well as respecting
the context. On the left beyond
the glazed wall is the rear of
the Eiserners Haus that Peter
Cook has referred to as 'stuff'.

Above
The upper gallery, where the
roof becomes a source of light.

Right
View from the mezzanine into
the upper gallery, showing the
first installation.

Cook in particular reacts against the tyranny of the norms that have governed art museums where the architecture is supposed to be neutral but actually imposes a dead hand on interpretation. He would not be distressed, one feels, if some curators and even a few artists reacted against the Kunsthaus's idiosyncrasies because, as someone with considerable curatorial experience, he wants the building to have free reign to provoke, intrigue, fascinate and even set visitors on some sort of path to interpret. The interaction between work and space, between the cat's cradle of competing ideas that make up contemporary culture, needs to have scope to come into effect.

These perceptions run through the design, perhaps most importantly accounting for the drama: Cook is a keen orchestral concert goer and is acutely sensitive to timing, placement and sequence as generators of meaning through their contingent interaction. But Cook's and Fournier's perceptions of contemporary art inform the entire approach to design as an interactive dialogue. Drawing on the intellectual resources available to them as professors at the Bartlett, their design emerged through a series of iterative sessions where drawings and discussions played an equal part, all circling around an intuitive sense of what felt right. Cook expresses fascination for apparent minutiae which actually turn out to have vital bearing on the final impression. How do you cope, he muses, with the point where a consciously contemporary art museum abuts the almost completely new replacement of a late-19th-century monument? Neither 'fish, flesh nor fowl', he prefers to leave it as 'stuff', the sort of anonymous cladding panels that compete neither with the drama of the blue-glass skin nor the reticence of the Eiserners Haus. It knows, in other words, which uniform to wear, and it is in this ability to be extraordinary without being disruptive that the Kunsthaus makes its most impressive impact. ∆

Dale Jones-Evans

The Water House, Sydney, 1997–2002
This renewed terrace house was gutted and rebuilt around a new circulation core and light-well. The design makes the most of a tapering site that is 6 metres in width at the front and narrows to 3 metres at the rear. A new sunken pool and floating veiled pavilion terminate the narrow site. There is a transition from the solid heritage-protected front to the transparent new rear elevation and the pool and screened gym beyond. At night, when the screen masks the gym beyond, there is little demarcation between inside and outside space. The night sky becomes a welcome presence: lights are reflected on the surface of the water, and turned into a mirror by the black-tiled pool surface – a surface that is broken up in lattices of shadow from the screen.

Leon van Schaik discovers an element of the sublime in the recent Sydney-based work of Melbourne-educated Dale Jones-Evans. An architecture of screens, which celebrates glittering surfaces and creates soft reflexive spaces, it is one that is sensitively attuned to the Sydney latitude.

The English language creates an illusion of seamlessly shared mental space across some widely disparate parts of the world. The British and their former colonies have special ways of denigrating their samenesses, but much that is different eludes definition, or even awareness, in verbal language. During my student years in England I recall a sniffy description of Australia as 'a desert surrounded by a suburb'. It was also referred to as 'a working man's paradise'. Both were intended as put-downs, though it is hard to see why these are unfortunate characteristics, unless one is pretending to be a landed aristocrat.

Sydney is different in ways that have defied architectural imaginations honed on architectural discourses from the north. Anglophone culture seems to be startled at finding itself at this latitude. But an attempt at sameness is what has been wrought by 200 years of settlement. For example, a mean, concrete, municipal pathway leads along the cliffs from Bronte to Bondi, and a grid of red-tiled roofs is combed to an untidy fringe of lawn, as if the Tasman Ocean is merely a real-estate awkwardness.

Brighton and Hove have done better. Consider Sydney's geography. In the northern hemisphere cities at the same latitude include Rabat, Beirut, Damascus, Baghdad, Xian, Osaka, Atlanta and Los Angeles. In the southern hemisphere, give or take a degree or two, Sydney shares, with Adelaide and Perth, the following cities: Cape Town, Buenos Aires, Santiago de Chile. The sight of rugby being played in drizzle in Sydney may suggest an element of familiarity, but this latitude is far more exotic than Melbourne's companion cities of Lisbon, Alicante, Athens and so on. There is an element of the sublime in Sydney that requires a fresh start for any Anglophone mentality but it is rarely addressed.

Recent works by architect Dale Jones-Evans are an exception to this denial, partly because he is not a local and is aware of how alien to Sydney is his Melbourne upbringing, and partly because – as a surfer rather than a yachtsman – he comes to the place through an immersive engagement in its sensuality. He is obsessed

Metalika, Sydney, 1999–2001
Night view showing how the connection to the street is maintained. The ground-level units are shops/offices. Screens are set at an angle to the face of the building to afford privacy to the penthouse suites, further screens project horizontally for sun shading, and balconies serve the same purposes for the maisonettes. The building employs an industrial aesthetic of off-

shutter concrete, polished for the floor, a chromed section of reinforcing rod for the door handle and lighting that makes reference to the artists Turrell and Flavin, both favourites of Jones-Evans.

with the endlessly forming fractal gauges of lattices of sunlight on the facets of waves, interspersed with flecks of white foam, a glittering surface that burns its way into the skin and eyes. And it is as a result of this obsession that Jones-Evans has begun to develop an architecture of screens.

In addition, the architect's research into the depth of surface led to his collaboration with Catalan artist Dani Marti, and somehow their partnership has tapped into a north African, southern Spanish sensibility which, at its apogee, has produced some of the finest architecture – an architecture that is completely attuned to its latitude and to the inclusive tolerance of the culture that nurtured it. As at Granada, this is an architecture that screens us from direct exposure to the elements yet, through a series of veilings, engages us with the shrillest presence of the veils at midday, their passing moods of morning and evening and the endless scalar shifts created through degrees of brightness. Some of these are threshold effects, brought about in plan: courtyards and cloisters shield us from the outside though at the same time always afford intense glimpses into the landscape. Others are screening

effects, weaving a protective distance between us and the outside world, creating soft reflexive spaces from which its dangerous beauty can be savoured.

This new approach was signalled in the Water House at Elizabeth Bay (1996–2001). The view from the rear of this elegantly renewed terrace house is funnelled towards an organically ordered screen of metal rods that projects from, and largely obscures, the gym that is cantilevered over the black swimming-pool. Shadows from this screen break across the walls of the outdoor space. Here, Jones-Evans has worked with black walls and water within the house to provide a welcome coolness during the day yet a space that sparkles with reflected light in the dark at night.

Horizontal and vertical grilles are prominent features of Jones-Evans's approach to apartment-block design in inner Sydney. In some instances, metal mesh accessways and balcony floors provide solutions to planning conundrums that have defeated more conventional arrangements. For example, in an early

The Art Wall, Sydney, 2000–03

A prow at the entry level shields the building from the street, cut back to afford views from the restaurant. The office floors above are sheathed in the laser-cut screen, and the building is surmounted with an artwork, a depiction of a work by one of Australia's finest Aboriginal artists, that Jones-Evans went to extraordinary lengths to secure. From inside the building, the lattice screens both soften and intensify the relationship between inside and out. They give privacy without separation, at the same time cutting down the glare.

Emily Kngwarreye, Alalgura Country, 1994

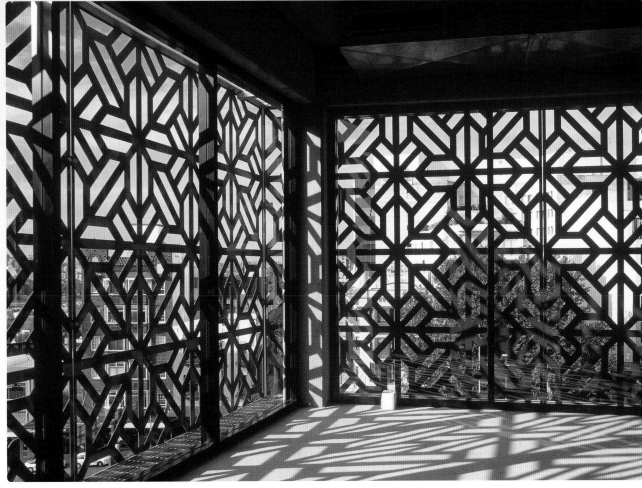

The Loft, King Street Wharf, Sydney, 2001–02
Top two images and plan
Loft is reached by a flight of stairs from the street. Toilets are tucked in behind a lattice light-wall that runs on behind the horseshoe bar. There is room for a moderate crush around the bar. Seating here is in formal sets, and patrons are seated and waited on by staff. There are views across the water from the south and west. The exit to the street is a stair designed for gracious departures into the night.

Bungalow 8, King Street Wharf, Sydney, 2001–02
Bottom image and plan
The Bungalow 8 plan concentrates the bar and toilets against the part-basement street wall. There is a broad crush space between the bar and the seating areas, and this can be closed off from the 'veranda' area with folding doors. This space has a lacquered bamboo ceiling, lit by basket-weave lights, and there is a translucent wall of light behind the bottles to the rear of the bar.

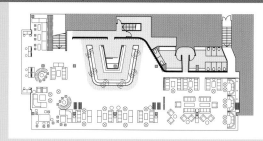

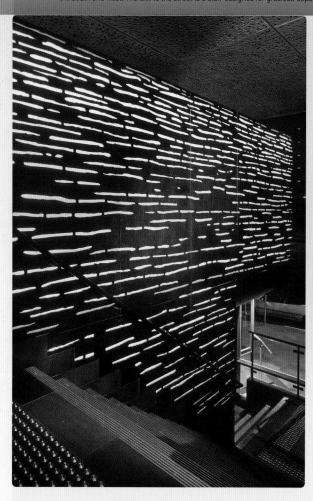

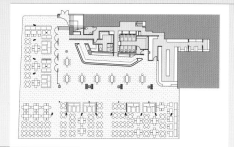

Red Box, Docklands, Melbourne, 2002–03
The screen is situated between two high-rise apartment buildings, and protects a dockside
promenade that steps down to the quayside. The pixilated weave plays with levels of
transparency, allowing glimpses through the complex overlapping patterns. It stretches over
the concave plan, giving the skin a textile-like quality.

project it was the realisation that external accessways could
be made by hanging mesh floors outside the building envelope
that rendered the development viable. And this concept was
also used at Metalika (2000–01), where the grilles were used
to provide an intimate connection to street life, providing both
light and view, and shading and privacy.

These hints of a new way of dealing with Sydney's psycho-
geography intensified as Jones-Evans began to work more
closely with Dani Marti, whose work weaves industrial
materials into fabrics of unexpectedly rich texture and depth.
The Art Wall project (2000–03) is a development on a site
overlooking 'The Cross', so exposed to this hub of nocturnal
activity and traffic that it had defied successful occupation for
decades. However, Jones-Evans has created a defensible zone
by making a steel prow that extends a deck from the entrance
at ground level so that it becomes a balcony for the first-floor
restaurant – a vantage point from which to view the busy street,
away from the bustling crowds. The balcony protects a lower-
level shop, and provides a cover for the pre-existing practice of
sleeping out against the building flank. Above the balcony level,
a laser-cut lattice screen covers four storeys of office space in
a continuous shield, protecting the privacy of those within and
providing a mediated connection to the busy scene outside.
The building is surmounted with a mural, derived from a

painting by Emily Kame Kngwarreye (1920–96) on licence
from her community in the Red Heart of Australia.

The architect's design here is a self-evident,
elementary solution to this difficult site. The voyeuristic
component of the local culture is perfectly catered for
and the liberal coexistence that characterised Arab
Spain and that is a distinguishing feature of Sydney's
culture is embedded in the form that allows for the
parade of style and the tolerance of difference that has
always attracted people to King's Cross. Yet this was the
first building here to use this architecture of screens
and prows.

Two large bars at King Street Wharf on the harbour,
the Loft and Bungalow 8 (2002–03), take this
architecture of screens and filtered light into the heart
of Sydney's dating scene. Bungalow 8, which the
architect deprecatingly describes as 'a South Pacific
taverna', opens onto the quay along its south and west
perimeter. The ceiling is made of black-lacquered split-
bamboo. The irregular concavities ripple light from
suspended lanterns that string out into the open
'veranda' seating area, and the bar is suffused with
soft light defused into the space from a translucent
wall fronted with bottles. Levels of illumination are
flatteringly dim and intimate. The bar is strung out
along the rear wall; the push here is to get the drinks
out into the clusters of people across the floor plane
and out under the night sky. Upstairs, in the more
exclusive Loft, patrons are met by a host or hostess
and guided to a sofa or to the bar, which is deeply
horseshoe to enable eye contact with others across
its depth. Every wall and ceiling surface seems to emit
light through lattice grilles. Light is bounced upwards
and diffused downwards by chandeliers along the bar,
giving an Arabian Nights effect. In an innovative
inversion of expectations, the leaving of this bar is
more celebrated than the arriving. A wall of light laid
in masonry strips at the exit stairs beckons to the
street – and life beyond.

The Loft gives pride of place to a Dani Marti weave,
created to match the laser-cut patterns designed by
Jones-Evans architects. This architect/artist interaction
has resulted in a number of collaborations, beginning
with the design of a suite of windscreens for Yarra's
Edge (2002–03), a docklands development in
Melbourne. All start with a weaving procedure in mind,
which is developed in the context of the specific
situation for each screen. Thus four concepts have
been developed – Red Box, Metalika, Pearl and Tanks
– which hint at future developments in this marriage
between research and practice.

Contemporaneous work in the office includes
Folded House (2002–03). This meticulous restoration
of a bungalow (the architect argued for its heritage
listing) benefits from all that Jones-Evans has learned

Folded House, Bronte, Australia, 2002–03
The section and elevation below show the existing four-room bungalow to the north, and the extensions to the south. A new stair leads to a new bedroom in the loft. The swimming pool is enclosed in a courtyard between the existing house and the new pavilion-like extension. This new entertaining area houses the cooking, dining and living zones. It features a horseshoe kitchen/bar, and has sliding glass doors that open to cross breezes, even if air-conditioned during the day. The thick forms of the bungalow roof are folded out into the casing for the new extension. The folded roof of the new extension affords privacy from an adjacent apartment block. The new striated fence at the base of the street entry becomes part of the landscaping.

about dimming down the effects of light. To be on the veranda, tucked in behind drab olive and black paintwork, standing on sandstone flags, looking down through this hooded space onto a long pool, is to feel the full relief of observing the world and its riot of light from a properly protected space. The rear of the house embraces a swimming pool and there is a dining terrace on the rear boundary. The deeply drawn-down hat of the house gives rise to the upturned prow of copper sheathing that covers the extension. As a prow this form serves the architect well at the Art Wall, but is less convincing as a folding extension of the bungalow roof form. Impressive though the spaces are, it feels as if the building stems from a pre-screen period of the architect's work. Many of the effects of the house would have been more easefully achieved in that mode. As it is, Annie Wilkes's almost totally green landscape will extend a shielding of growth around the currently unprotected glass walls.

Jones-Evans is an architect with a keen eye for the actualities of experience who avoids the prevailing tendency of Sydney architects to police taste in a Minimalist mode. The work that is emerging from his practice now promises to build on the exceptional reality of the latitude he has adopted. Elements of the object-obsessed formal culture of which he was once a part in his native Melbourne are still evident in his work, for example in Folded House. But the increasing emphasis on screens and surfaces, lighting for the sub-tropical night and the porous tolerant culture that Sydney epitomises, are signs of a more interesting architecture that is more to do with situating people in an environment than impressing them with its form.

This is emerging in Jones-Evans's current collaboration with an artist from a region of the world at home with the sensuality of latitude 34°. Too little is made of such collaborative researches in the understanding of intellectual change. In their early adulthood, Lorca and Dali spent a formative summer together. Lorca drew, Dali wrote. They sketched their shadows in the sand, the outline of one giving the profile of the other. The divisive political events that followed have obscured the fact that these written sketches were starting points for much of Lorca's later work, and the drawings foreshadow Dali's surrealism.

Many of Australia's best practices are made of such intimate creative exchange. Given the surreal quality of 200 years of Anglophone overlay on Sydney's 'Rabat', this particular collaboration seems be moving in a fruitful direction: Jones-Evans's intimate and dangerous engagement with the sea and light, and his intensely liberal social awareness, combine with Marti's tradition of the procedural practice of weaving. This may result in even more deeply latticed environments than those the architect has thus far created – environments that already transcend the tight boundaries of the usual Sydney Modernism. ⌂

Leon van Schaik is innovation professor of architecture at the Royal Melbourne Institute of Technology. He was ccommissioner for Australia in the Venice Architecture Biennale 2000, and was on the advisory board for the 2003 Netherlands Architecture Biennale. He writes for international architecture journals including *Architectural Design*, *Architectural Review Australia* and *Archis*.

Resumé
Dale Jones-Evans

1975 Completed a Bachelor of Fine Art and Design degree at the Caulfield Institute of Technology at Monash University, Victoria, Australia

1978 Completed a Bachelor of Architecture degree at the Royal Melbourne Institute of Technology, Victoria, Australia

1983–7 Directed Biltmoderne, an architectural and interior-design practice in Victoria, Australia

1985 Victorian RAIA Merit Award for Outstanding Architecture (Renovated Commercial Building) for Inflation nightclub

1987 Started Dale Jones-Evans Architecture

Victorian RAIA Merit Award for Outstanding Architecture (Residential New Building) for Choong House

1988 International Record Houses Award for Excellence in Planning and Design for Choong House

1991 Represented Australia at the 5th International Architecture Biennale in Venice, Italy

Gallery House wins National Royal Australian Institute of Architects National Robin Boyd Award for Most Outstanding Architecture and the Victorian RAIA Merit Award for Outstanding Residential Architecture

1994–6 Independently edited and published three editions of *Polis*, a journal that studies the development of cities from an urban geographic, planning and design perspective

1999 Privately developed Ann Street warehouse loft conversion

2001 Gold medal for excellence in print at the Nation Print awards for *Sea Gods*, a photographic book looking at Australia's seminal surfing characters, which was independently published and edited by Dale Jones-Evans

Roozen Residence wins West Australian RAIA Architecture Award (Single Residential) and receives a commendation for the BHP Metal Building Award

2002 BELLE House of the Year Award for Water House

Dulux Colour Award for Residential Interiors for Loft 6

Winner of Yarra's Edge Urban Art – Windscreen Art Installation Competition (Melbourne) in collaboration with artist Dani Marti

New South Wales RAIA Commendation Award (Single and Multiple Housing) for the Water House

2003 Privately developed Art Wall completed

Top
The digital model at an advanced stage of design development is useful for the study of
architectural components as well as for visualisation within the design team and in
communication with the client.

Bottom
The architects' concept sketch indicates
aspects of the building form's rationale.

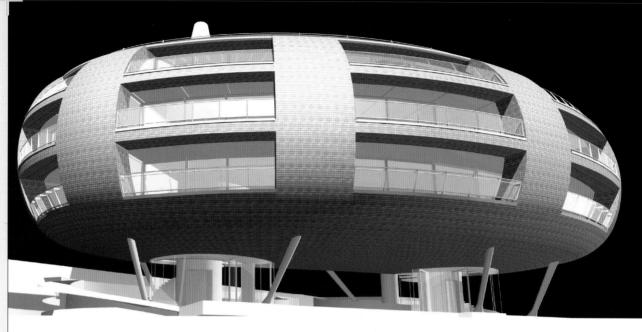

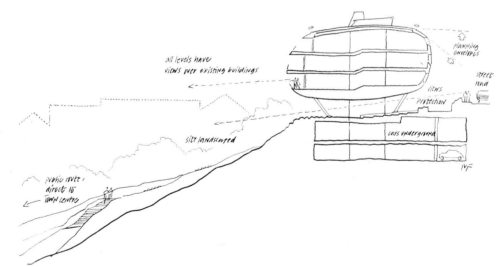

Blurring the Lines:

Case Studies of Current CAD/CAM Techniques

The Chesa Futura

Top left
The interactive plan and section manipulations give rise to a
reference surface that generates all subsequent solid geometries
by offsetting from it. The design consultants receive this surface
as their template for the various building systems' development.

Bottom left
The digital modelling begins with an arrangement of parametrically controllable
tangent arcs that can be manipulated to refine the architectural form and respond
to various performance requirements. The model at this stage is built by the
specialist modelling group by programming within the source code of the CAD
package. This initial investment of effort is then the basis of extensive collaborative
studies by the designers.

Geometry Method

Plan View   Section View

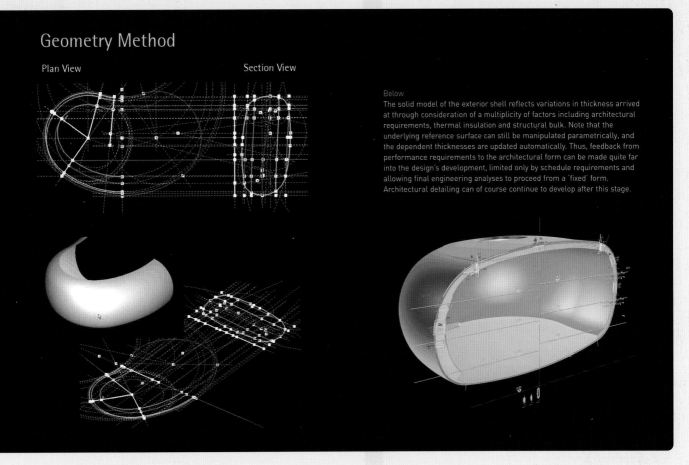

Below
The solid model of the exterior shell reflects variations in thickness arrived
at through consideration of a multiplicity of factors including architectural
requirements, thermal insulation and structural bulk. Note that the
underlying reference surface can still be manipulated parametrically, and
the dependent thicknesses are updated automatically. Thus, feedback from
performance requirements to the architectural form can be made quite far
into the design's development, limited only by schedule requirements and
allowing final engineering analyses to proceed from a 'fixed' form.
Architectural detailing can of course continue to develop after this stage.

André Chaszar describes how the design team on the Chesa Futura used a
combination of parametric modelling and digital structural and environmental
analyses, as well as CNC modelling and full-scale construction techniques,
to realise the Swiss apartment block's unique rounded 'pumpkin' form.

This unusually shaped apartment building located on a steeply
sloping site in St Moritz, Switzerland, is scheduled for
completion this year. Conceived by a team including Foster
& Partners and Arup, and Toscana AG as the local structural
consultant, the project relied extensively on digital techniques
for its design and analysis. Furthermore, a substantial portion
of the construction, comprising the building's wooden
structural and walling systems, was CNC fabricated from locally
harvested wood processed by contractor Holzbau Amann,
located in Germany. The project's main constructional features
are: a concrete foundation including garage and service
spaces; two concrete cores for circulation and services that
also give lateral stability to the structure; a steel-framed 'table'
structure that serves as the base for the apartment spaces and
stands on eight legs resting on the foundation; and a double-
curved wooden shell for the apartments that is punctured with
deep, rectangular openings forming balconies and giving shade
to the flat, recessed glazing. The project demonstrates the use
of parametric modelling, digital structural and environmental

engineering analyses, and CNC fabrication for design
study models as well as full-scale construction.

In seeking to develop a plan characterised by tight
systems integration and possessing a correspondingly
high degree of available space utilisation, the designers
found digital capabilities to be useful in numerous
respects, resulting in the following design process.
The architectural concept was sketched as a rounded
'pumpkin' form responding to, among other things,
sight lines, height restrictions, the developable area,
and the reduction of the building's bulk and envelope
area. In order to enable a manageable process of
refining this form, a parametric design method
commenced with definition of plan and sectional
curves constructed from circular arcs of varying radii
constrained to tangency at their junctions. The decision
to restrict curve segments to arcs stemmed from
a desire to maintain precisely developable offset
dimensions for the various assemblies as well as to

Right
The detailed digital model also includes internal systems whose coordination can thus be checked and their concepts easily communicated among the project participants.

Below left
Digital modelling of the primary structural system of the shell is part of an iterative loop with the structural analysis and design, with periodic checks against architectural requirements and other building systems as noted above.

Below right
Data from the CAD model is used at an advanced stage of design development to produce a very accurate and detailed physical model by CNC rapid prototyping. In general, Foster's practice prefers a design approach reliant on a variety of media including sketches, physical models, digital models and digitally generated drawings.

Bottom left
A detailed architectural CAD model of a segment of the shell aids study of the arrangement of its components, including the structural glue-laminated ribs, the stressed-skin insulated plywood panels, battens, shingles and fenestration assemblies.

Bottom right
The construction of a prototype wall segment provides proof of concept as well as an unprecedented opportunity to study detailing and constructibility issues. Although cladding mock-ups are fairly common practice in many countries for significant projects, the level of effort invested in them depends largely on the prevailing building culture. When it comes to innovative construction, such studies are invaluable even on small projects.

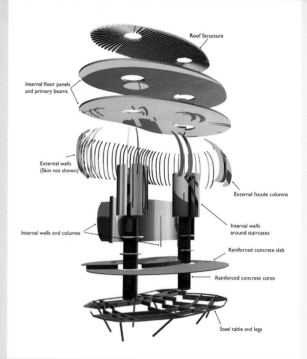

Roof Structure

Internal floor panels and primary beams

External walls (Skin not shown)

External facade columns

Internal walls and columns

Internal walls around staircases

Reinforced concrete slab

Reinforced concrete cores

Steel table and legs

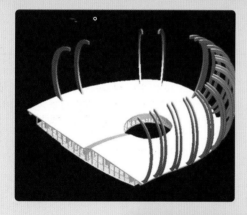

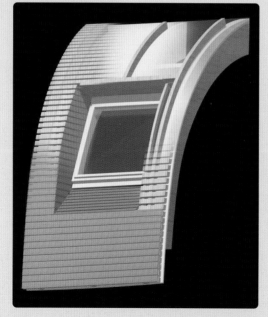

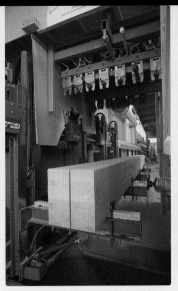

make the controlling form describable with relatively few data, making for easy and reliable transmission to other parties in the project team. Corresponding to this form, the construction scheme emerged from identification of the underlying polar coordinate geometries inherent in the plan, resulting in a segmental, radiating arrangement of primary structure and infill panels.

Given this 'design surface' and a desire to refine the framing, the designers benefited from a structural analysis showing that construction of the walls from stressed-skin panels could take advantage of the closed, relatively regular shape of the architectural form and result in shell action that allowed significant reduction of the primary structure's bulk and weight. Further development of the shell form in the 3-D parametric architectural model included refinement of the internal floor areas, ceiling heights and sight lines as well as definition of the surface as a series of patches constrained to tangency along the entirety of their joint boundaries. The roof and base were separated from the walls by two slightly inclined sectional planes, resulting in a ring beam and rain gutter at the top. 'Freezing' of the generating shell form by the architects at an early enough stage permitted finalisation of the engineering analyses while still allowing refinement of the architectural design through parametric manipulation of the various assemblies' offsets from the generating surface.

The comparatively low stiffness, weight and density of wood makes it suitable for high-speed, 3-D forming with a variety of tools, some of them digitally controlled. Primary structural elements were constructed as glue-laminated curved beams. Wood for the beams was harvested locally, from specially selected trees. The lumber sawn from these was dried and the slats planed and jointed with conventional high-capacity machines. Wall elements were designed as double-curved wood panels including glue-laminated elements, plywood skins and embedded insulation. The beam slats were laid up in a conventionally controlled

bending jig with glue, and clamped until cured. Next, one side of each glue-laminated member was planed so that it could rest evenly on the work surface for subsequent operations. The beams were then shaped by a CNC router with a variety of tool shapes, giving the required finished dimensions, tapering and the notches and other features required at joints. Some of the connection hardware was installed in the factory, and the pieces comprising the wall panels also assembled there. On site, the glue-laminated rib beams and ring beam were joined together and the wall panels subsequently inserted. In contrast, the walls' external cladding was accomplished with hand-cut shingles that give the desired appearance and weathering ability and conform well to the double-curved surface form.

This project thus demonstrates the capabilities of CAD in terms of describing complex forms and integration of systems, as well as the ability of parametric digital modelling to assimilate changes in particular aspects of the design geometry – for example, in response to external constraints such as regulations concerning the building's bulk – while preserving the overall relationships between the components. CAM milling of wooden elements exemplifies a process in which digital fabrication comprises a substantial portion of the work and requires relatively little further processing, in comparison with the cutting of sheet materials, for example, which require significant further assembly before they are complete. △

André Chaszar is a consulting engineer and contributing editor of △. This case study is the first in a series illustrating the concepts and techniques introduced in the 2003 volume's 'Blurring the Lines' articles on CAD/CAM in contemporary architecture. These and other articles are to be collected together in a new book, *Blurring the Lines: Computer-Aided Design and Manufacturing in Contemporary Architecture* (Wiley-Academy), to be published in 2005.

From Political Reportage to *Prêt-à-Porter*

Fashion Retail, by **Eleanor Curtis**, is about where fashion and architecture meet. It attempts to capture the exciting and vibrant design activity happening in fashion stores throughout the world. At the high end of fashion, stores are being refitted on an almost annual basis in a whole range of styles, from the purist Minimalism to the fantastical 1970s-inspired Futurism. In addition to the interiors, whole buildings have been conceived by some of the top-name architects for the biggest names in fashion, and to budgets that, only a decade ago, would have suited museums.

The first in a new series entitled 'Interior Angles', the book features work by Rem Koolhaas and Herzog & de Meuron for Prada, Renzo Piano for Hermes, and some incredible work for the Louis Vuitton stores by their in-house architectural team. Interior projects feature sumptuous Minimalist designs by Claudio Silvestrin and Gabellini, for Giorgio Armani and Jil Sander respectively, and cutting-edge designers such as Will Russell for Alexander McQueen and Universal Design Studio for Stella McCartney. The final chapter departs slightly to look at the evolution of the department store, with the new Selfridges in Birmingham by Future Systems as its centrepiece.

Directly following my guest-editorial of Δ *Club Culture*, *Fashion Retail* is my third book for Wiley-Academy and, like *Club Culture* and my first book *Hotel Interior Structures*, it examines design in the wider context of design identity. For example, *Hotel Interior Structures* scratched at the surface of the currently debated issues regarding how far interior design can inform lifestyle and the identity that it strives to give to new hotels such as those featured in the book. These issues were then expanded in Δ *Club Culture*, which looked at how architecture and interior design can give an exclusive edge to a club in order to attract certain types and reaffirm the identity of its members. And the latest of the publications, *Fashion Retail* focuses on where fashion meets architecture and examines the relationship of design and identity in the context of fashion stores.

In retrospect, since writing the book on hotel interiors five years ago, it has been incredible to witness the ever-intensifying promotion of 'lifestyle' through architecture and design – whether in the hotel lobby, the health club, the airline lounge or the fashion store.

My work on architecture and design – as a writer and photographer over the last ten years, as a freelance contributor to various journals and newspapers and, in the last seven years working closely with Wiley-Academy, began whilst I was living in Cairo in the mid-1990s and continued when I moved to Italy and then back to London. Although I do not always do all of the photography for my publications, working as a photographer has certainly always been a help in editing the images.

However, these projects represent only one of two strands of my work. The other falls under the broad category of 'international affairs' and is a world away from the creative efforts of architecture and design. My work in Cairo covered some aspects of the political issues in the Middle East, but mainly through the lens of urban design. I saw how urban plans were directly linked to the political policies of the day in the three major cities of the Middle East – Cairo, Jerusalem and Beirut. The urban developments were incredibly fast and aggressive, pouring concrete into the earth in order to ensure strong demographics for the future. It was both fascinating and shocking to see for myself what was happening.

My work in Angola, Southern Africa, in the late 1990s, however, changed my view on all things. I had originally gone out there to join my fiancé and to continue to work as a freelance writer and photographer for London, with the idea of doing some post-colonial architectural stories and perhaps some travel pieces. Instead, I was confronted by a nasty civil war that had blown up again just days before I arrived in late 1998. Knowing that facilities would be limited, I had taken with me a darkroom kit, and this became my lifesaver.

The war in Angola raged on for another four years, with oil and diamonds being used as the bargaining chips, and I began to take a deeper interest in the issues at stake. Angola was no longer on the maps of any Western newspapers and it therefore proved difficult to get feature stories out. This was an old civil war with its causes linked to the Cold War days. Nevertheless, I did manage to write features for some of the broadsheets back in London and sell a number of news stories too. I also pursued various photographic stories, one of which made the front page of *the Guardian*, that were to lead my work on Angola for a further three-and-half years.

My photographic studies of Angola in conflict resulted in an international photographic exhibition that was well sponsored, for example with photographic materials from Ilford. The images represented the full range of Angolan life as it was at the time – from war to oil rigs, to landscapes and architecture. It is a truly beautiful country with which I feel a personal link after developing friendships and knowledge of some of the more remote parts of the country. In the meantime, other lines of work developed as a result of my time in Angola, including photo-journalistic projects on landmines and the diamond industry, and some of these are still work-in-progress.

But how do the two strands of work – architecture and photojournalism – fit together? The mix has come about by accident more than design, and is a result of my own ideas of how the world goes round. There is no doubt that to work at both ends of the spectrum – one safe and creative, the other insecure and in a constant state of flux – is a privilege that constantly sharpens my views. One informs the other, giving me an appreciation of both worlds.

When returning to write about architecture and design after time 'in the field', I am always overwhelmed with an appreciation for the stability afforded us by our Western cultures that allows creative expression to manifest itself in many forms. I see how a history of political stability and, in some ways, predictability, gives artists and architects freedoms within which to create. The economic reasoning behind the commissioning of the architecture and design in question is also key to my analysis and provokes many interesting issues regarding the link between our built landscape and economic policies. The same question was applied for *Fashion Retail* when examining the commissioning of new architecture and design for the fashion houses – why at this particular point in time is fashion investing so much money into architecture?

This said, the production of art (and architecture) is not confined to stable societies. There are historical instances of extreme oppression and brutality from which has been born some of the most incredible literature of the age, despite being mostly restricted and often heavily censored. However, what is clear from experience is that when a society is dealing with a nasty civil conflict there is little time to talk about art and architecture. And without political stability and good governance there are no books on architecture to write. Space precludes a full discussion of this subject – of the relationship between art, architecture and politics – but I will end by saying that this subject is at the heart of my work. ∆

Middle
Girls playing skiprope, Kuito, Angola 2000

Bottom
Museum of Slavery, Luanda, Angola 2001

Neufert/Karle + Buxbaum
Ernst-Neufert-Bau, Darmstadt

Neufert/Karle + Buxbaum
Ernst-Neufert-Bau, Darmstadt
Klaus Honold

ISBN 3930698501 Hardback £24.00 60 pages
65 b/w and colour illustrations Published by
Edition Axel Menges, Stuttgart/London, 2003

Replanning and converting a listed building can be counted among the most difficult and yet interesting tasks for young architects, particularly when the building in question is of post-Second World War vintage and was designed by one of the most controversial 20th-century German architects.

This book, by German journalist Klaus Honold, has as its central theme the story of a social housing block originally designed for bachelors by Ernst Neufert from 1951 to 1955, and recently converted into a mixture of private luxury flats and social-housing units by Darmstadt-based architects Peter Karle and Ramona Buxbaum (2000–02).

Published as No 50 in the 'Opus' series of Edition Axel Menges, the book features an essay by Honold on the history and context of the bachelor's home past to present; a mini practice-profile of Karle Buxbaum Architects; a small section showing drawings of the original and present state of the building; and 30 pages of stunning colour photographs of the completed conversion. Individually, all of the parts of the book work well if considered on their own. However, unlike the main essay, which provides a concise chronological account of events, the remaining three parts – despite being beautifully presented – do not quite support the story that earlier on has been set up for the reader in such an effective way.

Honold's generally very informative text, 'With Neufert, against Neufert, without Neufert: the art of correction', briefly explores Darmstadt's architectural heritage and thus the setting for the bachelor's home, establishing some valuable biographical information on Neufert, his controversial history and the original design of the building, followed by the story of the conversion and a short introduction to the work of Karle and Buxbaum. The essay is well structured and an enjoyable read. There is, however, a lack of the kind of illustrations in the book that could emphasise the points the author is making, especially with regard to the new architectural intervention. Whilst Honold describes in some detail how the original design came about, and how Karle and Buxbaum skilfully went about the very difficult task of transforming a building which in its original state was as much criticised for its 'remorseless rationalism' as it was eventually admired for its uniqueness in Neufert's oeuvre, it would have been helpful to find more visual evidence and comparison of the before and after in a book concerning itself with the problem of how to fit the new into the old.

Thomas Eicken's brilliant photographs in the second half of the publication take the reader on a journey from outside into the building in its postconversion state, but any interior shots of the original Neufert-designed spaces are absent and there is only one preconversion exterior photograph of the building. Hence Karle's and Buxbaum's clever spatial play and the qualities and effects of their intervention are, I would suggest, not appropriately represented.

Similarly, there is a shortage of drawings documenting the two different stages of the project. The plans and sections by Neufert and those by Karle and Buxbaum are individually professional and legible, yet neither particularly underlines the qualities or shortcomings in Neufert's design nor supports Karle's and Buxbaum's masterful insertion of *Unité d'Habitation*-style flats into the existing listed shell of the building.

All that said, by touching on some very delicate issues such as the difficult biographical involvements of some of the postwar greats during the period from 1933 to 1945, this book, on the story of an important building by an architect with a patchy history, featuring the work of a thriving and ambitious young practice, does refreshingly stand out from the usual outbursts of vanity publishing that seem to have become the norm in the field of architectural monographs. ◬

Reviewed by Torsten Schmiedeknecht

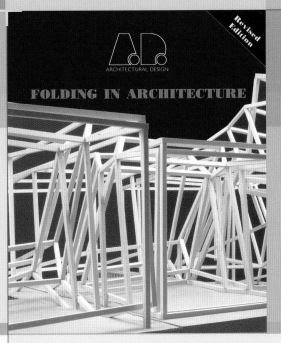

Folding to Non-Standard 1993–2003

In April 2004, Wiley-Academy published a new edition of Greg Lynn's seminal title of Æ, *Folding in Architecture*. Mario Carpo, who has written a substantial article for the preface of the new edition, considers the relevance of *Folding* against the backdrop of the recent Non-Standard Architectures exhibition at the Centre Pompidou in Paris.

The exhibition on Non-Standard Architectures (Centre Pompidou, Paris, December 2003 to March 2004) was in many ways a milestone, and the chances are it will be remembered as such. It set forth some of the technical paradigms of the new digital age in unequivocal terms: computer-based manufacturing can already mass-produce series of objects that are all (within some crucial limits) visually different from each other, and economies of scale no longer require the reproduction of identical parts. This is the opposite of the technical paradigm that came with the Industrial Revolution in the 19th century and was sublimated by architectural Modernism in the 20th century. Assembly lines in the computer age may deliver customised products at no additional cost: translate this into the metaphor of the *machine à habiter*, upgrade the metaphor from mechanical to computer-based technologies, and you will come to the inevitable conclusion that standardised architecture has lost all economic and technical reasons to exist.

However, the exhibition as well as the essays published in the accompanying catalogue present a more confusing picture. Visitors are likely to be dazzled by the diversity of the references, and many will leave the exhibition with a vague notion that 'non-standard' in architecture means all that is, was or ever will be round. But this is wrong. Non-standard defines a process of production, not the form of individual products. Non-standard production means that product 1 in a given series is different from product 2 in the same series, and not that product 1 and product 2 must be round – nor square, plump, flaccid or whatever.

In addition, the rise of the industrial standards and types in the 20th century (and the belated vindication of those who reacted against them in the course of the last hundred years) is only a part of the story. The repetition of identical part and the quest for identicality have been persistent issues throughout Western architectural history, particularly during the Renaissance. Conversely, the genealogy of the contemporary debate on non-standard architecture belongs mostly to much more recent developments in architectural theory that took place at the end, and not at the beginning, of the 20th century.

In many ways this is a whole new story, which started little more than 10 years ago. Among the protagonists of this *Nouvelle Vague*, the 1993 special issue of Æ, *Folding in Architecture*, now being reprinted with new prefaces, deserves special mention. Read in hindsight, *Folding* eloquently portrays that crucial moment of change, on the eve of the digital revolution, when the heritage of Deconstructivism and the Deleuzian infatuation, then pervasive in the US, briefly coalesced to create the cultural environment where computer-based design and manufacturing would soon take root and thrive. Theories on topological and non-standard architecture followed and replaced each other, yet the anticipatory character of that seminal publication is still striking. Laden with much noise that now sounds as if it came from another century – as it does – *Folding in Architecture* is already a chapter of history, but as such it recounts a crucial part of a narrative that at some point in the future must be written in full: the story of digitisation taking command. Æ

Mario Carpo is head of the Study Centre at the Canadian Center for Architecture in Montreal. He is also Robert Sterling Clark visiting professor of art history at Williams College, and associate professor of architectural history at the School of Architecture of Saint-Etienne, France.

Below
Map of the Potteries Thinkbelt showing main routes, transfer, faculty and housing
areas. The map was reproduced in *D* from *New Society*.

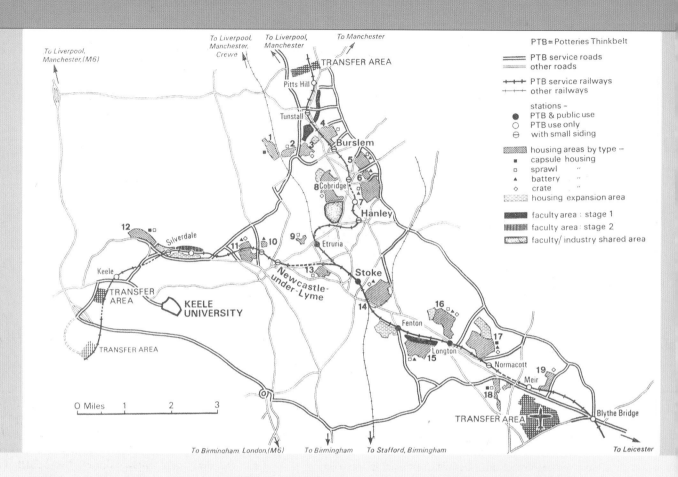

Supercrit#1 and #2

The Supercrit has been established by EXP – the new centre for experimental research in the Department of Architecture at the University of Westminster in London – as a regular new forum for discussing architectural projects and ideas. Samantha Hardingham, a research fellow at the school and part of the EXP team, describes the ground-breaking Potteries Thinkbelt Supercrit#1 and the forthcoming LAWUN-Invisible UniverCity Supercrit#2.

Experimental projects are at the core of architecture's thought and teaching. Used by its greatest practitioners to test and reinvent the way architecture is practised, they act as a laboratory of ideas for the building professions. EXP – the new architectural research centre at the University of Westminster – has been set up with the intention of running live projects, exhibitions, publications and debates, to support, disseminate, record and archive such work. The Supercrit series is at the centre of the programme. It invites architects and protagonists of key iconic and major ongoing projects to present their work for assessment and debate by a panel of international expert critics and an audience of students, practitioners and an interested public. Supercrits are open to all and are recorded for future study.

Supercrit#1

The Supercrit series was launched on 5 November 2003 with a debate on Cedric Price's 1966 Potteries Thinkbelt project. The project was to have been presented by Price (1934–2003) but due to his tragic and untimely death, Supercrit #1 instead became a key element of his three-day memorial event in London. The project was presented by Paul Barker, former editor of *New Society* (in which the project was first published in June 1966) and collaborator with Price on the Non-Plan project (1967), along with architectural historian and writer Jeremy Melvin, and Stephen Mullin, chief assistant on the Potteries Thinkbelt. The event was chaired by Emap publishing director, CABE commissioner and long-time friend Paul Finch. The

Below left
Axonometric of the Madeley Transfer Area (see map opposite). The rail–road link provides facilities for handling, assembly and construction of large-scale goods and equipment. Two workshop zones with adjustable high-level servicing and access are adjacent to conventional work areas capable of cellular variation, which in turn adjoin reception, public and amenities areas. Rising from the latter are the accommodation towers. These provide minimal hotel accommodation and are likely to be used by short- and medium-term visiting staff.

Below right
The Potteries Thinkbelt project was introduced in an article in *New Society* in June 1966 but was latterly to be given more comprehensive, illustrated coverage in △ in October the same year. The cover of that issue displayed what has become a key image for the project – a collage view from inside a train arriving at one of the transfer areas on the site.

audience discussion included Phyllis Lambert, head of the Canadian Center for Architecture, former △ technical editor Peter Murray, Archigram's Dennis Crompton, former RIBA president and Cedric Price Architects (CPA) employee Paul Hyett, Cedric Price student and co-architect of the Graz Kunsthaus Colin Fournier, film-maker Patrick Keiller, artist Bruce McLean, former chief planner of Southwark Fred Manson, developer Roger Zogolovitch, and Price's companion, actress Eleanor Bron.

Britain in the 1960s, Paul Barker explained, was 'anything goes': interest rates were low, unemployment almost unheard-of and – except in the London docks and other early postindustrial areas such as the Staffordshire potteries – there was 'always money from somewhere'. Variations on themes of politics and education were obsessions of the time. The school-leaving age had been raised, and Harold Wilson claimed his most major achievement was establishing the Open University – astonishing in an era that abolished capital punishment, legalised homosexuality and changed race relations. 'It was a decade of optimism – things could be improved, and quickly.' And in this society Price was 'both optimist and an iconoclast'.

Price's relationship to contemporary architecture, Jeremy Melvin continued, was one of 'extraordinarily perceptive detachment'. Architects of the 1960s were building university megastructures everywhere ('like the one we're in,' he added, gesturing at the massive, extruded studio-mezzanine level section of the University of Westminster). But Price's take on the pressure for higher education and housing was not to design another new town, but rather a prototype of what we now call brownfield regeneration; nor (as everyone else was doing) to put a new university on the outskirts of towns that had narrowly missed getting them in the Middle Ages, for

example Canterbury, Coventry or York. The Potteries Thinkbelt project, he said, was about 'devising new communities and engaging with what was really there'.

The site, Stephen Mullin explained, was an 'utterly gutted landscape' criss-crossed with rails, canals and roads, 'a dreadful place called Etruria' with 'a terrible lack of housing' – a 'foretaste of Thatcher'. The other project in the CPA office at the time was the Fun Palace, which was interlinked in escaping the static constraints of the building. 'Cedric saw the provision of enclosures as being slightly secondary to place.' Facilities were loaded on flatbeds, running on trains, folded out in facility zones, with three large transfer areas for goods and services. The really important thing though, Mullin explained, was the housing: none of it 'student housing' since everyone would be a student, and not 'balanced' but allowed to happen naturally, with four different types – Crate (multistorey steel frame), Battery (single-storey), Capsule (airstream type) and Sprawl – the names chosen particularly, Mullin explained, to 'get up the noses of the RIBA and the Royal Town Planning Institute'.

Given its memorial status, it is not surprising that Supercrit's analysis was laced with much praise. But Barker's suggestion that the Potteries Thinkbelt was 'a critique, not an on-the-ground scheme', set off endless debate. Paul Finch called the project 'not building – better than building – challenging the idea of what you're building and why'. Peter Murray commented: 'I'm depressed to think it was not meant as an on-the-ground scheme. We desperately wanted this to be built.' Paul Hyett said 'Cedric always wanted to build' – but everyone agreed it

Top
Diagram of all housing types, showing applications to various site conditions:
total number of housing units provided: 32,372.

Bottom
LAWUN-Invisible UniverCity: pages from the project scrapbook. 'It is worth
exploring the things that destroy the purpose of one's own effort.' – Cedric
Price in conversation with David Greene, 2003.

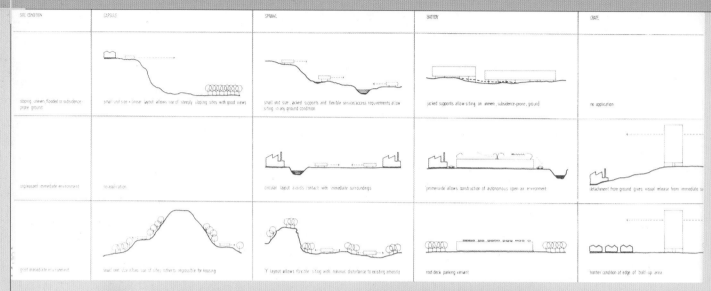

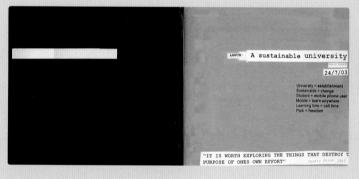

would only be on his terms. Fred Manson raised the idea of the
anti-aesthetic/poetics of Cedric's work: 'It's extraordinary that the
end result is poetic through an utterly rational method.' Mullin
added: 'All of Cedric's buildings have very strong aesthetics –
casual, accretive and functionally descriptive – the whole idea
is aesthetically rounded in a way few projects are.'

The project seems – as does all Price's work – hugely
predictive and more relevant than ever now that we're living
in the circumstances he always managed to foresee. Finch,
among many others, commented that 'Cedric is as fresh and
relevant today as ever,' and went on to say that this example
of ''regeneration + education + transport + reuse' remained an
untapped model for the UK's current urban problems. Of Price's
Canadian Centre for Architecture competition scheme for the
west side of New York, which did not win first prize, Phyllis
Lambert said: 'I'm quite embarrassed that we chose to build.
The idea of not building – of not having to build – will take hold.
But I don't know when.'

The last word, though, went to Cedric, as read out by Samantha
Hardingham. In relation to the Potteries Thinkbelt 'it is what
makes sense to *you* now, what is useful to *you* today ...' ⌂

Samantha Hardingham is research fellow at the School for Architecture and the Built Environment,
University of Westminster. She is the author of *Cedric Price Opera* (Wiley-Academy 2003). In the
1990s, the successful ellipsis series launched its eponymous grey guides with her title *London:
A Guide to Recent Architecture*, which has gone into several editions and has recently been
republished in a new format by Batsford.

Supercrit#1
Supercrit#1 was supported by the University of Westminster,
Architectural Design (Wiley-Academy), the CCA and the Slade Breakfast Club.

Supercrit#2
LAWUN-Invisble UniverCity is a current research project by Archigram member
Professor David Greene in association with EXP. The project is an investigation into
the relationship between mobile technology and higher education, a sustainable
out-in-the-open university. Throughout his career, David Greene has been
motivated by a fascination for the way that rapid developments in technology
(in its many guises, from robot to mobile phone to cash-point machine) impact
upon and interact with the more slow-to-move built and natural environment.

LAWUN = Locally Available World Unseen Networks (1969) was conceived as
part of David Greene's electric garden of delights, which also included Rockplug
and Logplug. In this most recent investigation, entitled the Invisible UniverCity,
Greene proposes that we think about the future uses of mobile technology in
relation to higher education, in particular a school of architecture. The project
explores the interactivity between the accepted definition of 'university' as a fixed
place for knowledge transfer and conversation, and the potential for mobile wire-
free technology to deliver teaching and learning in a truly extramural context.

Individuals engaged in consulting on and developing the project include Pete
Silver and Will McLean from the University of Westminster, Jason Bruges Studio,
Usman Haque, Chris Leung, Jon Goodbun of WaG Architecture, Theodore
Spyropoulos, Vasili Stroumpakos, librarian at the University of Syracuse Jana
Bradley, textiles expert based at the Royal College of Art Susannah Handley,
Richard Rogers Partnership's Mike Davies (formerly one of Greene's students)
and Chris Dawson, Liza Fior of Muf, and mobile-phone network company Orange.

The project continues as a 'live laboratory' at the University of Westminster
with a forthcoming presentation of work-in-progress taking place in June 2004
during Architecture Week, and to coincide with the end-of-the-year student
shows and the Archigram exhibition at the Design Museum (April to July 2004).
The project will be the subject of a Supercrit#2 in November 2004.

EXP is coordinated by Dr Kester Rattenbury with research fellows Dr David
Lawrence and Samantha Hardingham.

AD Book Club
Architectural Design

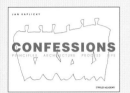

Confessions: Principles Architecture Process Life
Jan Kaplicky

Confessions offers an insight into the mind of Future Systems architect Jan Kaplicky – his ideas, opinions and sources of inspiration. With an equal balance of images and textual observations, it is both visually and mentally engaging, and is an incredibly personal and honest account.

0-471-49541-7; 204pp; August 2002; Paperback; £24.95 £14.97

The Four States of Architecture
Hanrahan + Meyers Architects

The first book to chart the talent of exceptional New York firm, Hanrahan + Meyers, with support, via written contributions, from key figures such as Robert Stern and Bernard Tschumi

0-471-49652-9; 128pp; April 2002; Paperback; £24.95 £14.97

Sustaining Architecture in the Anti-Machine Age
Ian Abley

This book brings together contributions from a range of architects, journalists, academics and consultants, approaching sustainability from a wide variety of viewpoints. Each chapter includes a robust, lively text, illustrated with carefully chosen exemplar projects.

0-471-48660-4; 240pp January 2002; Paperback; £19.99 £11.99

First House
Christian Bjone

Covers the first works of a group of key architects who were teaching and/or studying at Harvard between the late 1930s and the early 1950s. Includes first houses by Gropius and Breuer, Ulrich Franzen, Philip Johnson, Paul Rudolph and IM Pei

"...beautifully produced clever and thoughtful..."
—The Twentieth-Century Society Newsletter

0-470-84538-4; 224pp; April 2002; Hardback; £39.95 £23.97

Archi-toons: Funniness, Comedy and Delight
Richard T Bynum

Explore the lighter side of architecture with this volume of humorous cartoons from the internationally renowned architect and popular cartoonist and illustrator Rick Bynum. These cartoons take a quirky, witty, insightful and sometimes irreverent look at the world of design, architecture and construction.

0-470-85406-5; 128pp; April 2003; Paperback; £9.99 £6.00

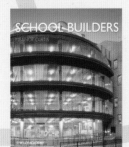

School Builders
Eleanor Curtis

School Builders provides a fascinating overview of the latest developments in school design from around the world. Packed with construction methods, case studies, outstanding imagery and technical plans, it offers an indispensable guide for planning and designing school buildings, from primary through to high schools.

0-471-62377-6; 224pp; January 2003; Hardback; £50.00 £30.00

Encyclopaedia of Architectural Technology
Jacqueline Glass

A comprehensive guide to architectural technology, that encompasses every aspect of modern construction. Including several hundred entries in alphabetical order with diagrams and illustrations, this is an essential guide for the architect and student alike

"More than a mere dictionary of architectural terms...a useful reference tome with a detailed explanation of many key terms."
—Architects Journal

0-471-88559-2; 360pp; February 2002; Hardback; £60.00 £36.00

Below
Designing from the inside out, Gehry strove to rid the gallery of its Achilles heel – its maze-like circulation. A long-overdue shift in the main entrance restores the axial alignment with the classically arched Walker Court. Inside the newly skylit space, a spiralling Baroque staircase twists its way through the roof to the contemporary galleries. Seen less as circulation and more as a meeting place, the curvaceous staircase is actually the only gesture that speaks the Gehry language.

A Sort of Homecoming: The Art Gallery of Ontario

Reporting on Frank Gehry's new Art Gallery of Ontario, **Sean Stanwick** raises important questions about architectural expectations. What happens, for instance, when Gehry chooses to pull the plug on the Bilbao effect on his home turf?

What started as a conversation in early 2002 led to an emotional homecoming for architect Frank Gehry as he unveiled his plans for 'Transformation AGO', the make-over of the Art Gallery of Ontario in Toronto. And while the aim is to strengthen the relationships between the gallery and the city, Gehry has delivered a mixed bag that questions the fundamental expectations when hiring the world's most famous 'starchitect'.

Founded in 1900 by local citizens, the AGO is currently the tenth-largest art museum in North America and holds the world's largest public collection of works by British sculptor Henry Moore. The renovation will add 75,000 new square feet and expand the total gallery viewing space by 40 per cent. The catalyst for the $195 million renovation is a $98 million donation from Canadian business tycoon Kenneth Thomson, plus $48 million in government funding. The remainder is expected to come from private donations and fund-raising. Of the money donated by Thomson, $50 million in cash is earmarked for the expansion project, with the rest consisting of more than 2,000 pieces of Canadian and European art from Thomson's private collection, including *Massacre of the Innocents* by Peter Paul Rubens.

While his first major Canadian commission bears few resemblances to the Gehry lexicon, it is certainly

Below
From the mandate to transform the experience of art, a titanium-and-glass scrim delicately
slants and twists as it runs the entire length of the gallery's 600-foot facade. Gehry chose
titanium for its unique ability to turn golden on cloudy and rainy days – characteristic of
Toronto's weather, he remembers these fondly. Behind, a 450-foot sculpture gallery provides
views to the street below and easy access to the main galleries beyond.

not wanting for architectural drama. Stretching over 600 feet
along the entire northern facade is a swooping titanium-and-
glass scrim that slants and twists along its length. Behind
the screen, a linear sculpture gallery provides exterior views
and way-finding to the main galleries beyond. At ground
level, the space of the street is engaged through a bookshop,
members' lounge and theatre. To the south, overlooking
Grange Park, is a four-storey rectilinear box. Also in tinted
glass and titanium, it will house a hosting facility,
contemporary galleries and a dining hall. Recounting
childhood memories of the country's weather, Gehry said he
chose titanium for its unique ability to turn golden on cloudy
and rainy days. Ground-breaking is set for early 2005 with
completion anticipated in 2007.

What is ironic is that the man best known for distorting the
conventions of modern architecture has delivered a scheme that
is an exercise in clarity. Designed from the inside out, 'the big
change,' he says, 'is how it reforms and rebuilds the institution.'
It is no secret that the maze-like circulation was the gallery's
Achilles heel so Gehry's much-needed shift in the main entrance,
which restores the axial alignment with Walker Court, the historic
heart of the gallery, is well received. Clearly from the hand of
Gehry, a spiralling Baroque staircase on this same axis twists
its way to the contemporary galleries above. Slightly awkward
in its relationship to the existing court, the curvaceous staircase
is actually the only gesture that speaks the Gehry language.

One of the project's strengths is that it is actually a
relatively modest urban insertion that understands its
civic role in Toronto's current architectural renaissance
– a collective urban transformation led by other notable
projects including Libeskind's Crystal for the Royal
Ontario Museum, a massive building campaign by the
University of Toronto featuring works by Morphosis and
Norman Foster, the College of Art by Will Alsop and the
Opera House by Diamond and Schmitt. However, this
brings to light the most salient aspect of the project,
the obvious urban comparisons to Bilbao and the
fundamental question it raises: Was Gehry courted for
his ability to solve the functional issues, or were we
more interested in the brand that he has become?

Granted there is a certain kerb-appeal to the slick
Constructivist facade, and while Gehry concedes there
is still much work to be done, expectations were
extremely high that he would design something in at
least the same vernacular as Bilbao. A glance at the
many schematic design iterations on display shows
that he was clearly exploring billowing metallic options.
Unfortunately, the realities of the project clearly took
precedence – the gallery simply did not have the capital
funding for such a grandiose gesture.

But to suggest that Toronto will be excluded from the
media attention that comes with the Frank Gehry brand
is unrealistic, as not all Gehry buildings are shimmering
blobs of titanium. Nevertheless, while the building is
clearly functional, many are still disillusioned, left
wondering whether we are to applaud his departure
from the clichés of object building or mourn the loss
of our own Bilbao effect?

Perhaps the shroud of secrecy and the lack of public
involvement fuelled the feelings of estrangement from
the development process and led to the mixed reviews.
Interestingly, the city was reminded as early as
November 2002 that it would not be similar to Bilbao.
It seems we should have heeded the warnings and
asked ourselves the obvious question: Could the
gallery have realised far more 'architecture' for the
same budget but without the Gehry moniker?

Expectations notwithstanding, many are confident
the scheme will support the city's architectural
renaissance and enhance the art experience. It comes
as cold comfort, though, that in the homecoming of
the world's most celebrated architect, funded by the
country's richest man, it was the realities of money
and not our expectations for grandeur that played a
significant role in diluting the architectural bravura. Δ

Based in Toronto, Sean Stanwick is a regular contributor to Δ who has a particular
interest in urban design and the themed spectacular. He has contributed to
Sustaining Architecture in the Anti-Machine Age, and is currently writing Interior
Angles – Wine by Design and Interior Angles – Lofty Ideas [all for Wiley-Academy].
He is an instructor with the Royal Architectural Institute of Canada and is currently
a design architect with Farrow Partnership Architects.

Subscribe Now

As an influential and prestigious architectural publication, *Architectural Design* has an almost unrivalled reputation worldwide. Published bimonthly, it successfully combines the currency and topicality of a newsstand journal with the editorial rigour and design qualities of a book. Consistently at the forefront of cultural thought and design since the 1960s, it has time and again proved provocative and inspirational'– inspiring theoretical, creative and technological advances. Prominent in the 1980s for the part it played in Postmodernism and then in Deconstruction, ⚁ has recently taken a pioneering role in the technological revolution of the 1990s. With groundbreaking titles dealing with cyberspace and hypersurface architecture, it has pursued the conceptual and critical implications of high-end computer software and virtual realities. ⚁

⚁ Architectural Design

SUBSCRIPTION RATES 2004
Institutional Rate: UK £175
Personal Rate: UK £99
Discount Student* Rate: UK £70
OUTSIDE UK
Institutional Rate: US $270
Personal Rate: US $155
Student* Rate: US $110

*Proof of studentship will be required when placing an order. Prices reflect rates for a 2002 subscription and are subject to change without notice.

TO SUBSCRIBE
Phone your credit card order:
+44 (0)1243 843 828

Fax your credit card order to:
+44 (0)1243 770 432

Email your credit card order to:
cs-journals@wiley.co.uk

Post your credit card or cheque order to:
John Wiley & Sons Ltd.
Journals Administration Department
1 Oldlands Way
Bognor Regis
West Sussex PO22 9SA
UK

Please include your postal delivery address with your order.

All ⚁ volumes are available individually. To place an order please write to:
John Wiley & Sons Ltd
Customer Services
1 Oldlands Way
Bognor Regis
West Sussex PO22 9SA

Please quote the ISBN number of the issue(s) you are ordering.

⚁ is available to purchase on both a subscription basis and as individual volumes

○ I wish to subscribe to ⚁ *Architectural Design* at the **Institutional rate of £175.**

○ I wish to subscribe to ⚁ *Architectural Design* at the **Personal rate of £99.**

○ I wish to subscribe to ⚁ *Architectural Design* at the **Student rate of £70.**

○ ⚁ *Architectural Design* is available to individuals on either a calendar year or rolling annual basis; Institutional subscriptions are only available on a calendar year basis. Tick this box if you would like your Personal or Student subscription on a rolling annual basis.

○ Payment enclosed by Cheque/Money order/Drafts.

Value/Currency £/US$ [   ]

○ Please charge £/US$ [   ] to my credit card.
Account number:

[ ][ ][ ][ ][ ][ ][ ][ ][ ][ ][ ][ ][ ][ ][ ][ ][ ]

Expiry date:

[ ][ ][ ][ ][ ][ ]

Card: Visa/Amex/Mastercard/Eurocard *(delete as applicable)*

Cardholder's signature [   ]

Cardholder's name [   ]

Address [   ]

[   ]

[   ] Post/Zip Code [   ]

Recipient's name [   ]

Address [   ]

[   ]

[   ] Post/Zip Code [   ]

I would like to buy the following issues at £22.50 each:

○ ⚁ 169 *Emergence*, Michael Hensel, Achim Menges + Michael Weinstock

○ ⚁ 168 *Extreme Sites*, Deborah Gans + Claire Weisz

○ ⚁ 167 *Property Development*, David Sokol

○ ⚁ 166 *Club Culture*, Eleanor Curtis

○ ⚁ 165 *Urban Flashes Asia*, Nicholas Boyarsky + Peter Lang

○ ⚁ 164 *Home Front: New Developments in Housing*, Lucy Bullivant

○ ⚁ 163 *Art + Architecture*, Ivan Margolius

○ ⚁ 162 *Surface Consciousness*, Mark Taylor

○ ⚁ 161 *Off the Radar*, Brian Carter + Annette LeCuyer

○ ⚁ 160 *Food + Architecture*, Karen A Franck

○ ⚁ 159 *Versioning in Architecture*, SHoP

○ ⚁ 158 *Furniture + Architecture*, Edwin Heathcote

○ ⚁ 157 *Reflexive Architecture*, Neil Spiller

○ ⚁ 156 *Poetics in Architecture*, Leon van Schaik

○ ⚁ 155 *Contemporary Techniques in Architecture*, Ali Rahim

○ ⚁ 154 *Fame and Architecture*, J. Chance and T. Schmiedeknecht

○ ⚁ 153 *Looking Back in Envy*, Jan Kaplicky

○ ⚁ 152 *Green Architecture*, Brian Edwards

○ ⚁ 151 *New Babylonians*, Iain Borden + Sandy McCreery

○ ⚁ 150 *Architecture + Animation*, Bob Fear

○ ⚁ 149 *Young Blood*, Neil Spiller

○ ⚁ 148 *Fashion and Architecture*, Martin Pawley

○ ⚁ 147 *The Tragic in Architecture*, Richard Patterson

○ ⚁ 146 *The Transformable House*, Jonathan Bell and Sally Godwin

○ ⚁ 145 *Contemporary Processes in Architecture*, Ali Rahim

○ ⚁ 144 *Space Architecture*, Dr Rachel Armstrong

○ ⚁ 143 *Architecture and Film II*, Bob Fear